THE
WEALTH
SOLUTION

Bringing Structure to
Your Financial Life

THIRD EDITION

Steven Atkinson, Joni Clark & Alex Potts

Afterword by DR. HARRY M. MARKOWITZ,
Recipient of the Nobel Prize in Economic Sciences

IRN: B 13-050

Third edition

Printed in the United States of America

Library of Congress Control Number: 2011920405

Paperback ISBN: 978-0-9858087-1-6

Hardcover ISBN: 978-0-9858087-3-0

For his friendship, his courage and his passion

for empowering investors through education,

this book is dedicated to the memory of

Gordon Murray.

Foreword

"Wealth is the ability to fully experience life."

— Henry David Thoreau

Since we published our first edition in May 2011 the response from individuals and families — as well as the wealth advisors they work with — has been extremely positive.

We really had one goal in writing this book: to help you achieve your long-term financial goals.

There's no doubt that the past few years have been challenging for many investors. It can be difficult to know the right decisions to make when there are so many "experts" who all seem to contradict each other.

But it really doesn't need to be so confusing. And investing definitely shouldn't feel like a game of chance.

I believe, without hesitation, that the strategy we employ in this book and in our business can be the right approach for many investors.

This realization was something I came to more than 20 years ago.

After Iraq invaded Kuwait in 1990, one of the outside mutual fund managers we were working with decided to suddenly move from stocks to cash. This was in a mutual fund that was supposed to maintain a steady and consistent discipline. But the manager made the move anyway, made it too late, and put our carefully developed portfolio allocations at risk.

It was a real "light bulb" moment for me, as it showed me the importance of long-term investing in defined, consistent asset classes, instead of actively managed mutual funds where the actions of a single manager can compromise your long-term plans.

As you read this book, I think you'll find yourself realizing that maybe there is another way to think about investing — one that offers you a more methodical and long-term approach as opposed to trying to figure out which "hot" stocks to buy and when to buy them.

As one of the great advocates for the way we invest, Gene Fama, Jr., once put it: *"Investing is like a bar of soap — the more you touch it, the less you have."*

One of my favorite ways to think about investing is very simple — really, everything you need to know about capitalism and how investing works can be found in a $2 cup of coffee.

From a farmer harvesting a coffee tree, to the shipping company that transports the coffee beans, to the corner coffee store where you get your morning coffee (in a cup made by a paper mill), countless companies and individuals are working hard to make possible your $2 cup of coffee — at a profit to each of them and happily enjoyed by you.

So if you find yourself concerned about stock market headlines, think of it this way…when you invest, you are really investing in nothing less than the long-term potential of capitalism powered by the value of human innovation. It is as simple as a $2 cup of coffee.

Whether you are an experienced investor with a multi-million dollar portfolio, or someone just starting out, you will find that the majority of the concepts in this book can apply to you.

After all, wealth is about much more than just how much money you make. It's being able to make choices for yourself and your family — and in the process enjoy the impact you can make in helping others.

Perhaps, as you read the following pages, you will have a "light bulb" moment of your own.

> — ALEX POTTS
> *CEO,* Loring Ward

Table of Contents

CHAPTER 1

A Framework for Financial Success

"Being rich is having money; being wealthy is having time."

— Henry Ward Beecher

A few years ago, a friend who worked as an executive at a huge technology firm in Silicon Valley found herself in a dismal financial situation — facing an enormous tax bill on stock option gains that, for a variety of reasons, never found their way to her bottom line. Suddenly, instead of enjoying a well-earned retirement — replete with sunny vacations and free time to spend with friends and family — she was forced to continue working in order to help rebuild the wealth that she never should have lost in the first place.

Her story is troubling and all too common, even for sophisticated investors. We've seen too many similar financial missteps over the years. Many investors never reach their most important goals — not because they aren't smart or don't make the effort, but because they don't have a successful plan to help them get there. As a result, they end up compromising not just their own futures, but the futures of their families.

Our goal in writing this book is to give you the tools you need to make smarter financial decisions and avoid the mistakes that too often trip up investors.

Saving and investing to reach your financial goals can often seem like a huge challenge. And chances are, you're at least a little uncertain about whether the decisions you're making with your money in a variety of key areas — from investing to minimizing taxes to paying for a child's education — are the right decisions.

You are the reason why we've written this book. It will give you a simple framework to help you make better, more informed financial decisions.

Before we get started, we need to acknowledge an important fact. It's become harder than ever to navigate through the increasing complexity of our lives and ensure that we are making consistently wise decisions with our money. Achieving financial goals was challenging enough even before the so-called "Great Recession" and the tremendous upheaval in the financial markets. In the wake of those events, many investors feel more confused and uncertain about their futures and are unsure how to get back on the right track.

When we first sat down together to discuss the idea of writing a book to help investors, it was in late December 2009 — the tail end of a decade that saw the worst 10-year return for the Dow Jones Industrial Average since the 1930s. During that time, many investors watched their hard-earned savings plummet in value. They questioned their approach to investing, and worried that they would have to delay or forgo some of their important life objectives such as a comfortable retirement or leaving a legacy to their children. This fear is not easily forgotten.

But it's important to recognize another fact: There is a process that can help simplify your life and your finances and help ensure that you're making the smartest possible decisions about your money day in and day out. What's more, it's a process used by some of the most successful families in America to manage their wealth.

This process — which we call *360 Wealth Management* — is what this book is all about. As you'll discover, this is a fundamentally different approach from those used by many investors (including most financial advisors and investment professionals). It is designed to help you understand not only your financial issues, but the personal, family and social issues that impact and influence financial decisions.

360 Wealth Management: **An Overview**

The *360 Wealth Management* process is consultative, comprehensive and grounded in data, research and analysis.

- **Consultative**. This process begins with what is most important to you personally. What are your most deeply held values and goals? This will then, in turn, help you identify and clarify the specific financial goals that will have the greatest impact for you and your family. By beginning with this step, all your future financial decisions can be made "with a purpose" — that is, within the context of your life. This method is distinctly different from other approaches, in that it steers you to make decisions based not on events in the markets or the economy but on your values and the steps you should take toward your unique goals.

  It is not concerned with picking hot stocks or trying to beat the market. Instead, this approach encourages you to answer an extremely powerful question: "What should I be doing with my money to provide the life I want most?"

  Adopting this approach puts tremendous purpose behind your financial decisions. Your time frame and perspective are immeasurably broadened, and you no longer have to worry about what the stock market is doing today or this month or even this year. Your plan is based around a desired long-term outcome — not short-term noise.

- **Comprehensive.** Many investors focus only on one aspect of their finances — often their investment portfolios or 401(k) accounts. Of course, smart investment choices are crucial to achieving long-term financial goals such as a secure retirement. But for nearly all of us, there are other vital issues that need to be addressed. Depending on your circumstances, these issues could range from saving for college to helping aging parents meet health care needs to providing for children and heirs to supporting your favorite non-profit organizations and causes.

360 Wealth Management addresses the full range of issues that investors and their families face, and it ties everything together seamlessly, so that the individual components — investments, insurance, wills and so on — always work together effectively. Having access to an advisor that collaborates with experts in ancillary fields (such as tax, legal and insurance) ensures that all advice given is well-coordinated.

- **Grounded in data, research and analysis.** Based on decades of financial data and research, this rational and practical approach helps investors avoid making rash, emotional decisions that could derail their plans and make it harder for them to reach their goals. For example, many investors in the wake of the financial crisis of 2008 and 2009 became fearful of investing in the financial markets. But we know from history that markets have tended to work in the long run — despite the occasional crisis.

In order to fully take advantage of *360 Wealth Management* and to make the most of its benefits, we encourage you to work in partnership with a financial advisor who uses the type of approach we outline in this book.

In our experience, we have found that investors tend to end up in a much stronger financial position when they enlist a professional whose job is to stay acutely focused on their clients' needs and goals at all times.

We believe that working in partnership with the right kind of financial advisor offers a much smoother path to achieving your financial goals.

Why You Need *360 Wealth Management*

The term "wealth management" may seem a little off-putting if you don't think of yourself as particularly wealthy. The truth is, you don't have to be among the super-rich to make the wealth management process a successful and important part of your life. We all face numerous financial issues, challenges and choices, from paying for today's bills to funding goals that might be decades away. These concerns won't solve themselves or go away if you ignore them. By disregarding them, you're simply asking for fate to make the decisions for you.

Making smart, rational choices about your finances can help you build the life you want for yourself and your family — regardless of whether you have $100,000 or $20 million. So ask yourself: Do you want to create a plan to address financial issues or do you want to leave it all to chance?

We think the answer is obvious. You have an obligation to make wise choices about your wealth. Your wealth can create a world of good — for yourself, your spouse, your children, grandchildren and beyond. So whether or not you "feel" wealthy isn't the point. In the end, your wealth can be a tremendously positive force in many, many lives. But you have to take proper care of it to make all that happen.

We'd like to show you how.

CHAPTER 2

The Key Challenges Facing Today's Investors

To understand how *360 Wealth Management* may help you achieve financial success, it's necessary to first recognize the most significant issues affecting investors today.

Chances are you're finding it more challenging than ever these days to manage your increasingly complex financial situation. But the sooner you determine where you are now and where you want to be in the future, the sooner you can set out to build a plan that tackles the major issues you face.

For more than two decades, we have worked closely with hundreds of top financial advisors who together serve thousands of investors. Our experience has taught us that investors today generally share six major concerns:

Concern 1: Preserving Wealth in Retirement

How are you going to grow and preserve your wealth so that you have the money required to meet your needs and fulfill your goals — not just today, but for decades to come?

The vast majority, regardless of their level of wealth, are concerned about preserving their wealth so they will have enough money throughout retirement.

Few of us want to be forced to downsize our lifestyles. And yet, many investors are not financially positioned to maintain their lifestyles during retirement — especially when you consider the challenges that today's pre-retirees and retirees must contend with. For example:

- **Inflation's impact.** Rising prices can decimate your savings and your ability to preserve wealth throughout your golden years. Assuming the long-term historical annual inflation rate of around 3%, an annual fixed income of $100,000 would be worth just $86,000 in five years and only about $40,000 in 30 years. A new car that costs $25,000 today would soar to more than $60,000 in 30 years. And if inflation runs at a much higher rate than normal for an extended period — a real concern given the huge amount of government spending that has occurred in recent years — the goal of wealth preservation throughout retirement could become even tougher to achieve.

- **Rising life expectancies.** Thanks to continued advances in health care, American seniors are living 50% longer than they were in the 1930s. According to the Centers for Disease Control, a 65-year-old can now expect to live another 19 years, on average.[1] For a 65-year-old married couple, there's a 49% chance that one of them will live to 90 and a 23% chance that one will reach 95.[2] While that is certainly good news, it also means that you will need to make your money last much longer.

- **Soaring health care costs.** The cost of health care has been rising at a much faster pace than the overall rate of inflation. This should be of particular concern to aging investors who are more likely than younger Americans to consume substantial amounts of health care. What's more, Medicare might only cover about 50% of a typical retiree's medical expenses. Consider that seniors age 65 and over spend an average of $4,888 per person annually for deductibles, copayments, premiums and other health care costs not covered by insurance, according to the most recent National Health Expenditure Survey.[3] That amount is more than two times the amount spent by average non-elderly adults. And the largest expenditures occurred among those 85 and older. According to the Employee Benefit Research Institute (EBRI), a retired couple age 65 would need approximately $283,000 to have a 90% chance of covering their out-of-pocket health care expenses in retirement.[4]

- **A weakening Social Security system.** It's no secret that Social Security has long been in trouble, but a look at the numbers is particularly sobering. 2010 was the first year in recent memory when the Social Security Fund paid out more in benefits than it collected in taxes. This deficit continues to this day, and based on current projections, the Social Security Trust Funds are scheduled to be depleted by 2033, according to the Social Security Administration.[5]

- **The diminished role of pensions.** Retirement has become a largely self-funded venture, as evidenced by the fact that just 32% of workers today participate in some type of defined benefit (pension) plan. That's down from a full 84% in 1980, according to EBRI. These days, the majority of workers (53%) participate in defined contribution plans — such as 401(k)s.[6]

- **Taking care of kids and parents.** According to the Pew Research Center, 15% of Americans ages 40 to 60 are raising a child while also caring for at least one aged parent. In addition, among those who have at least one living parent age 65 or older, roughly one-third say they have given their parent or parents financial support in the past year.[7]

---

1 Center for Disease Control and Prevention, "National Vital Statistics Reports," Vol. 60, No. 04, 2010.

2 Society of Actuaries based on 2010 Social Security tables with 1% mortality improvement.

3 "National Health Expenditure Data: Personal Health Care Spending by Age Group and Source Of Payment, Calendar Year 2004," Centers for Medicare and Medicaid Services.

4 'Funding Savings Needed for Health Expenses For Persons Eligible for Medicare," EBRI Issue Brief, Vol. 33, No. 10, October 2012.

5 "The 2012 Annual Report Of The Board Of Trustees Of The Federal Old-Age And Survivors Insurance And Federal Disability Insurance Trust Funds," Social Security Administration, April 25, 2012.

6 EBRI Databook on Employee Benefits, updated April 2011, Employee Benefits Research Institute.

7 "The Sandwich Generation — Rising Financial Burdens for Middle-Aged Americans," Pew Research Center, 2013.

The end result: Too many investors face a higher level of uncertainty about their future prospects than their parents and grandparents did. In the wake of that uncertainty, you simply have to be smarter, plan better and question many of the assumptions long-held by previous generations and many in the financial services industry. We believe that traditional "rules of thumb" advice such as needing 70% of your working income during retirement cannot be taken as gospel anymore. Your retirement plan needs to reflect the realities of the world today and in the future.

Concern 2: Minimizing Taxes

You've probably heard the adage that "it's not what you make, it's what you keep that counts." Not surprisingly, taxes are a major concern for most investors.

That concern is well founded, as taxes can significantly erode your ability to grow and preserve wealth. A $1 investment in stocks back in 1926 would have grown, before taxes, to $3,533 at the end of 2012 — but just $712 on an after-tax basis.[8]

There's cause for additional concern. Taxes during the past decade or so have been hovering at relatively low levels, but may be set to rise. Trying to predict tax code changes is a risky bet, of course. But you need to be aware that higher taxes across the board could be on their way — and at the very least, build sufficient flexibility into your plan so you can make adjustments should your tax situation change. The good news: You can take steps to minimize the taxes you pay and keep more of what is yours by using a variety of techniques that will be explored later.

Concern 3: Effective Estate and Gift Transfer

The ancient Chinese adage that "wealth never survives three generations" seems equally applicable today. A major concern for many investors is ensuring that their heirs, parents, children and grandchildren are well provided for in accordance with their wishes. And yet, our experience is that most investors don't have an estate plan — and many of those who do have outdated plans. Even more troubling: 61% of all American adults don't even have a will, according to a 2013 Harris Interactive study.[9]

Many investors don't take the appropriate actions in this key area because they assume they don't possess enough wealth to necessitate estate planning. Regardless of your net worth, the ability to ensure that your assets go where you want them to has numerous and important potential implications — from being able to help a child or grandchild go to college to ensuring the continuity of a family-owned business to simply avoiding probate. Take college tuition, for example. College education expenses have risen at a rate of more than 5% annually during the past decade, according to the College Board.[10] That means a child born today could need over $250,000 to attend a four-year public college in 2032 — more than triple today's college costs.

Passing on wealth and using it to benefit your heirs as you see fit requires the implementation of the right strategies for your goals and situation. As you'll see later, those strategies might include everything from correct titling of assets to smart gifting strategies and trusts designed to provide maximum benefits to a spouse, family members or charities.

Concern 4: Wealth and Income Protection

A significant number of investors today are worried about keeping wealth safe from potential creditors, litigants, children's spouses and potential ex-spouses, as well as from catastrophic loss. They also want to be sure that their loved ones are protected in the wake of major health problems or other unforeseen events.

In today's highly litigious culture, nearly everyone needs to consider the possibility of being sued. Increasingly, investors are realizing the importance of confronting some tough questions:

- What would happen if I were the victim of a lawsuit?

- What would happen if one of my children married a "gold digger," then divorced and was sued for a large sum?

8 Morningstar, Inc. 2013.

9 http://www.harrisinteractive.com/vault/2013_MAWMPressRelease.pdf

10 "Trends in College Pricing 2012," The College Board.

- What would happen if one of my children were in an accident in my car or someone suffered an injury in my home?
- What if a major disability prevented me from working and generating an income for my family?
- What if I end up needing to live in a nursing home or require home health care services?

Strategies aimed at wealth protection can motivate creditors to settle, decrease the possibility of being sued or minimize the financial impact of a judgment. Trusts and insurance can also play a role in protecting your wealth and income from an unexpected hardship.

Concern 5: Charitable Gifting

Charitable gifting is also very important to many investors. From direct gifts to formal gifting structures like donor advised funds and private family foundations, many investors are looking to ensure that their money is being used by their chosen charities to make an impact on the issues they care about most.

Simultaneously, these investors want to make sure that their philanthropic goals don't conflict with their ability to secure a comfortable retirement for themselves and leave a legacy for their families.

Concern 6: Finding High-Quality Financial Advice

For decades, much of Wall Street and the financial services industry have been driven by a sales-oriented culture that stressed pushing products instead of providing comprehensive solutions.

This concern reached a peak during the market downturn of 2008 and 2009 fueled by the revelation of the largest Ponzi scheme in history, and the fact that the largest investment firms in the world suffered tremendous losses from bad investment decisions they made on their own behalf. All of this created a significant and still-growing sense of dissatisfaction in, and distrust of, the financial services industry among many investors.

We recognize that many of you are looking for financial guidance and assistance. With that in mind, we've included a chapter in this book to help you find professionals who offer objective advice and who act only in the best interests of their clients. The good news is that during the past decade or so, more and more advisors have begun adopting a more comprehensive process such as that discussed in the following pages. If you choose to work with an advisor, you may find great benefit in using the guidelines and best practices in this book.

By focusing on life issues as they relate to financial issues, you can be assured that the decisions you make are in agreement with your overall goals.

CHAPTER 3

The *360 Wealth Management* Solution

A disciplined process can help you make prudent decisions toward achieving your most important goals.

But what exactly do we mean by *360 Wealth Management*? The term "wealth management" has become a buzzword in recent years. Financial advisors of all types are now calling themselves "wealth managers" and claiming to offer wealth management services. Unfortunately, many of these advisors are wealth managers in name only — after all, the title "wealth manager" sounds much more impressive than "stockbroker."

We believe that wealth management is not a term open to interpretation or multiple definitions. In order to benefit from true wealth management, you need to make sure you're actually bringing together financial professionals who possess the capabilities and expertise to address your biggest financial challenges and goals.

360 Wealth Management Defined

At its core, this philosophy is grounded in your values, beliefs and life goals, and it builds on these to address each specific area of your finances, employing professionals who have expertise in these specific areas (i.e. tax planning, estate planning, risk management, etc.).

This process stands in stark contrast to how most investors operate today. The vast majority of investors tend to address financial goals like college and estate planning on an ad hoc basis — treating these issues as separate concerns. These investors don't understand that the complex issues they face are often deeply interconnected and must be managed in a coordinated manner. Usually, issues are dealt with only as they arise, and typically just enough information is gathered to implement the particular solution to the problem at hand.

360 Wealth Management should be thought of as a detailed, three-part blueprint guiding all your decisions, ensuring that they all work together.

360 Wealth Management accomplishes this in three ways:

1. **A formal, consultative process** to gain a detailed understanding of your deepest values and goals. This process helps ensure that your financial issues are discussed in conjunction with your key life objectives.

2. **Customized solutions designed to fit your specific needs and goals.** The range of services and tools involved in crafting wealth management solutions might include insurance, estate planning, business planning and retirement planning.

3. **Collaboration with other professional advisors.** Work closely — and in a coordinated manner — with trusted advisors to identify potential issues, implement solutions and regularly monitor your overall financial situation.

Broadly, this blueprint incorporates all the main components of wealth management:

- **Investment management** takes into account your goals, your time frame for achieving them, and how comfortable you are taking risks. It is the foundation upon which a comprehensive wealth management solution is created.

- **Advanced planning** addresses the entire range of financial issues beyond investments in four primary areas: wealth enhancement, wealth transfer, wealth protection and charitable gifting.

- **Relationship management** consists of a network of experts who will be involved in providing you with solutions to your full range of financial issues.

To organize your thinking and approach to wealth management, you can use this formula:

360 Wealth Management = **investment management + advanced planning + relationship management**

Investors rarely take this type of coordinated and comprehensive approach with their finances. This is why wealth management is so important: It requires you to think through the full range of the financial challenges you and your family face, and develop optimal solutions that work in a coordinated manner. Whether you act as your own wealth manager or work collaboratively with a professional wealth advisor, you will gain a tremendous advantage over other investors who take a less disciplined, ad hoc approach.

The Wealth Management Consultative Process

Advisors who adopt a comprehensive wealth management approach have a formal structure they utilize in order to ensure consistency in their client interactions. Generally speaking, advisors will have a series of meetings with clients along the following lines:

1. **The Discovery Meeting.** The basis for any wealth management process is effective discovery. We believe that this must go far beyond the usual financial questions or simple data gathering. Discovery should not only seek to understand your financial issues, but also the personal, family and social issues that impact and influence your decisions. Until advisors understand your life issues, they will not be in a position to provide effective financial advice.

2. **The Investment Plan Meeting.** At this meeting, the wealth advisor presents a detailed series of investment recommendations based on the information uncovered during the Discovery Meeting.

A well-crafted investment plan can help you avoid making long-term investment decisions based on emotional responses to short-term or one-time events. Each investment plan should include these seven important areas of discussion:

- **Your long-term goals, objectives and values.** Long-term goals can consist of anything from early retirement to purchasing a new home to achieving financial independence. These goals are the foundation upon which your investment plan will be based.

- **Your expected time horizon.** Your time horizon consists of the length of time your portfolio is expected to remain invested. For example, a 65-year-old retiree should plan for a potential time horizon of at least 30 years.

- **Your comfort with risk.** It is important to understand the amount of risk you are willing and able to tolerate during your investment time horizon. In designing your portfolio, your advisor will help you determine your financial risk tolerance as well as your emotional risk tolerance (the amount of loss that you can accept without acting on your emotions and making hasty, unconsidered changes to your investment plan).

- **Investment methodology.** We firmly believe that investors are best served by using low-cost investment vehicles designed to work with markets — not against them.

- **Rebalancing or making periodic adjustments to your investment plan.** Part of keeping your investment plan on track involves making regular adjustments to your investments. We will explain more about rebalancing in the next chapter.

- **Monitoring and reporting.** Your goals won't remain static over time — they'll change as your life changes. That's why it's important to regularly monitor your investment plan to ensure it reflects where you are today and where you want to be in the future.

3. **Commitment Meeting.** It's important to consider the proposed investment plan thoroughly before committing to work with a wealth advisor. After you have reviewed the plan carefully, ask questions and voice any concerns before you decide whether to move forward.

4. **The 45-Day Follow-up Meeting.** This meeting allows your wealth advisor to help you understand and organize the financial paperwork involved in working together. It's also an opportunity to review any initial concerns and questions. In addition, your wealth advisor may discuss which advanced planning areas to focus on, and determine which outside experts to bring into future discussions.

5. **Regular Progress Meetings**. In these meetings, you'll review the steps you've taken toward accomplishing your various goals and make any necessary adjustments based on changes in your personal, professional or financial situation. This is also the forum to discuss priorities and objectives to be accomplished prior to the next scheduled meeting.

The Discovery Meeting

The Discovery Meeting enables you to identify all that is truly important to you in six key areas of your life. Your answers to the types of questions below will help enable you to develop an all-encompassing picture of your life goals so that all solutions and advice are made in conjunction with your unique situation.

1. **Vision & Values.** What do you want to accomplish with the money you have? As you think about your life, what kinds of things are most important to you? When you think about retirement, what vision comes to mind?

2. **Health.** What concerns you about either your health or the health of your spouse or family? What changes do you see occurring in your family health situation that should be taken into consideration? What plans have you put into place to protect your lifestyle or family in the event of a major health issue?

3. **Work & Relationships.** What do you like most about your work? What else would you like to do if you didn't have your current job? Do you have any plans to work after you retire, either for pay or as a volunteer?

4. **Family.** What family issues should we consider in creating your plan? Will caregiving be an issue for you at some point in the future? Who else in your family will be directly impacted by the plans we put into place?

5. **Lifestyle.** How do you like to spend your free time? If you had more time, how would you use it? How much would you like to travel in the future?

6. **Financial Comfort.** When you think about the future, what kind of things are you most concerned about? What are the biggest mistakes that you feel you make with your money? What needs to happen to make you feel comfortable about your financial situation?

If you have a spouse or partner, he or she should be equally involved in this discussion. Many couples have differing values, priorities or interests. Such differences need to be recognized so that you have a better understanding and appreciation of each other — and so that the plan you create can be effective in meeting your collective goals.

If you currently work with one or more financial advisors, you are probably aware that most use some type of fact-finding process in the first meeting. However, you may also have noticed that these questions usually focus entirely on your portfolio and net worth. In contrast, note that none of the six Discovery areas above concerns money. They are focused on helping you (and your wealth advisor) better understand what life issues are important to you.

Exhibit 3.1: Areas of Discovery

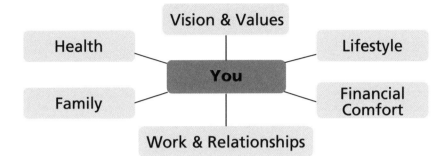

Of the six categories that make up the "Areas of Discovery" above, we believe the most important is the one representing your vision and values.

Values represent one of the core motivations for everything we do in our lives, and have a profound impact on every important decision we make, from what we do for a living to whom we marry to how we spend our free time — in short, they make us who we are. For example, if you're a parent you probably value your children above almost everything else in the world. As a result, you want to protect them, to educate them well and to set them onto a smooth path in life. Values run the gamut from the basic — such as security, financial freedom and not having to worry about paying the bills — to deeper issues like family, community, faith and reasons for being.

As important as values are, however, most of us are not particularly good at articulating them. The Discovery Meeting can help you uncover and clarify your core values.

In the following chapters, we'll explore each of the three main components of *360 Wealth Management* — investment management, advanced planning and relationship management — in more detail.

CHAPTER 4

The Investment Management Process: An Overview

Investment management is the foundation of almost every successful wealth management plan. While not everyone needs to worry about minimizing estate taxes or effective charitable giving strategies, all investors need to be sure they have enough money to live comfortably — both today and in the future.

Over the course of the next five chapters, we will review the key principles used by many prudent investors to guide their decisions. For example:

1. **Beating the market is virtually impossible, but capital markets work.** Strategies like trying to pick winning individual stocks or timing when to get in and out of the stock market have consistently failed to give investors an edge over the long term. However, the power of capitalism and free markets means that it is not unreasonable for investors to expect stock prices — as a whole — to gradually rise over time.

2. **Risk and return are related.** Academic evidence suggests that there are some risks worth taking so that investors can potentially generate stronger returns in their portfolios.

3. **Effective diversification can reduce volatility.** It's impossible to know with certainty when one type of investment will outperform all others and when it will underperform. Effective diversification helps ensure that your portfolio is not over-exposed to any single

investment category that is performing poorly at a given moment. The result: Your portfolio should experience more consistent returns from year to year instead of more dramatic swings in value — which, in turn, could enable your investments to build greater wealth for you over the long run.

4. **Building an ideal portfolio depends on each investor's comfort level with risk and investment preferences.** The right portfolio for you depends on your goals, income needs and time horizon. You'll also need to consider factors such as your feelings about market volatility, your reaction to potential declines in the value of your portfolio, and the types of investments that you are more comfortable owning in pursuit of your objectives.

5. **A disciplined long-term perspective is the key to staying on track and realizing your key financial goals.** Once your portfolio is created, let it do its job. That means staying invested instead of trying to time market movements, avoiding unnecessary trading and shutting down the many emotional and behavioral reactions to economic and market developments that can lead to costly mistakes. You can maintain your disciplined approach by taking advantage of resources such as Investment Policy Statements (see Chapter 8) to help stay on track.

Each of the investment categories in your portfolio behave differently and may react to market and economic environments in different ways. This is the very source of the potential benefits of diversification — the tendency of returns on different investments to offset each other over time. A portfolio that holds assets that do not perform similarly should experience less overall volatility and a smoother ride over time.

Ironically, this can also be a source of risk. The dissimilar performance of asset classes may also change the integrity of your asset mix because each asset drifts (in different direction or magnitude) depending on the market environment. As some assets appreciate in value and others lose value, your portfolio's allocation changes. Before you know it, your asset mix may be very different from its original composition. You could even end up with a completely different portfolio, with a return and risk profile inconsistent with your investment goals and preferences.

That is why, once you design a portfolio to match your current investment goals and risk tolerance, it is important to preserve its structural integrity. And one of the most effective tools for managing the risk of asset drift is *rebalancing*.

We've all heard the investing adage that we should "buy low, sell high." This is exactly what rebalancing does, taking money from assets that have performed well and reinvesting in assets that haven't.

Rebalancing does not guarantee greater returns over every period, but it helps reduce portfolio risk and may deliver better risk-adjusted returns over time.

While some of the information contained in the following chapters will no doubt be familiar — some may surprise you. By the end, we believe you will understand what it takes to build and maintain an investment plan that maximizes your chances of achieving your goals.

CHAPTER 5

Why Markets Work

Few things are more exciting to investors than the prospect of beating the stock market. If you can pick the right stocks and navigate your way successfully in and out of various market sectors at the right times, or find money managers to do the job for you, you'll generate outsized returns that will get you to your goals faster and help you achieve the lifestyle you desire. Not to mention that you'll get to brag to your friends and associates about the fortune you're making.

It's a wonderful and highly-appealing idea. Unfortunately, it suffers from a fatal flaw: History suggests that it's virtually impossible for even experienced money managers to beat the market consistently. We believe that by attempting to do so, you could put your financial dreams, goals and wealth at greater risk over time.

We realize that this probably isn't the first time you've been told that your chances of beating the market are extremely slim. We find that most investors understand and believe this on some level. But beating the market is such a tempting proposition that it's easy to forget. And when the markets run into trouble — as they did in recent years — there's always a resurgence of the idea that "things have changed" or "it's different this time," which causes many investors to look for ways to try and outperform the market as a whole.

Very few sources of information take the time to explain how financial markets work. In this chapter, we'll show you that the markets are incredibly difficult to beat, and, more importantly, why.

Our point is not simply to show that attempts to beat the market are largely futile. We believe that you don't need to beat the market to enjoy success as an investor. In fact, we think that the alternative approach — capturing the market's rates of return offered by each asset class — may help put you in a stronger position to address the major challenges you face and achieve the meaningful goals you've set for yourself.

Active Management vs. Passive Management

One of the fundamental choices you need to make about investing is whether you believe in an active or passive management style. Active management embraces the idea that you can beat the markets consistently. With an active management approach, fund managers actively buy and sell investments based on which ones they believe will perform best. In contrast, passive management's goal is to earn the same annual return as the markets. Since no one really knows which investments will do best or worst, passive managers rely on diversity and a long-term approach.

Who wouldn't want to outperform the market? Certainly many investors and money managers devote a great deal of time and energy trying. But long-term historical data boils down to one inescapable conclusion: Trying to outperform the stock market's overall rate of return by actively trading stocks or engaging in market timing has rarely succeeded over the long run.

Consider some of the most recent evidence from what has become a huge body of research over the years:

- **Active managers fail to prove success or skill in outperforming the market.** A recent study by Standard & Poor's Index vs. Active Group (SPIVA) found that the majority of active managers, across a variety of asset classes, failed to beat their benchmarks (see Exhibit 5.1).

Exhibit 5.1: Percentage of Active Funds that Failed to Beat Their Index (2008–2012)

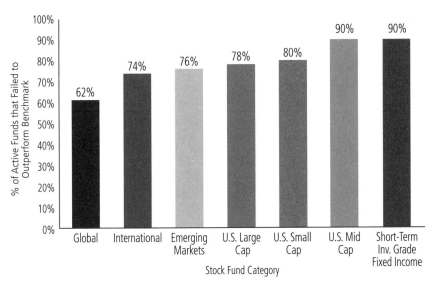

Source: Standard & Poor's Indices Versus Active Funds Scorecard (SPIVA), year end 2012. Index used for comparison: U.S. Large Cap – S&P 500 Index; U.S. Mid Cap – S&P MidCap 400 Index; U.S. Small Cap – S&P SmallCap 600 Index; Global Funds – S&P Global 1200 Index; International – S&P 700 Index; Emerging Markets – S&P/IFCI Composite; Short-Term Inv. Grade Fixed Income – Barclays 1-3 Year Government/Credit Index. Outperformance is based upon equal weight fund counts. For illustrative purposes only. Index returns do not include payment of any sales charges or fees an investor would pay to purchase the securities they represent. Such costs would lower performance. Past performance is not an indication of future results. Standard & Poor's®, S&P®, S&P 500®, S&P MidCap 400®, S&P SmallCap 600® and SPIVA® are registered trademarks of Standard & Poor's Financial Services LLC.

With the majority of active managers failing to beat the respective asset class index, finding a skillful manager that can outperform consistently would be akin to finding a needle in a haystack. As shown in Exhibit 5.2, even the managers who outperform over long periods of time do so by chance rather than by skill.

Exhibit 5.2: Percentage of Active Managers Who Outperform Due to Skill

Universe of Active Mutual Fund Managers 1975 – 2006

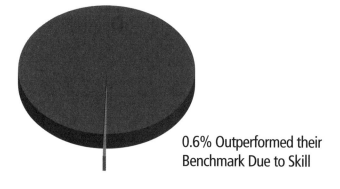

0.6% Outperformed their
Benchmark Due to Skill

In this 2008 research study[11] — perhaps the most comprehensive ever performed — a team of professors used advanced statistical analysis to evaluate the performance of active mutual funds. They looked at fund performance over a 32-year period, from 1975-2006.

The study concluded that after expenses, only 0.6% (1 in 160) of active mutual funds actually outperformed the market through the money managers' skill. The study concluded that this low number *"can't eliminate the possibility that the few [funds] that did were merely false positives."* In other words, they were just lucky.

Recent research, conducted by Eugene Fama of the University of Chicago and Kenneth French of Dartmouth, further supports these findings of luck versus skill.[12] In their research, they found that managers of actively managed funds, as a whole, possess only enough skill to cover their trading costs. Fama and French conducted 10,000 simulations of the effect of luck on fund returns and found that, *"The challenge is to distinguish skill from luck. Given the multitude of funds, many have extreme returns by chance."*

Despite the existence of these lucky few outliers, Fama and French concluded that very few fund managers have superior enough skills to beat their indices once costs were taken into consideration.

The research is further evidence that the majority of strong performing managers are simply lucky rather than skillful traders, and that top-performing managers are unlikely to noticeably outperform large index funds in the future.

The evidence leads to three conclusions:

1. Historically, it has been extremely difficult for most active management strategies to outperform the market over time.

2. Most active managers have also failed to demonstrate skill versus luck when they have outperformed the market.

3. A successful investment experience is not dependent on outperforming the market.

These points are especially important to keep in mind. After all, many of your most important goals in life are a decade or more away — such as ensuring that you have enough money to see you through a retirement that could last 20 or 30 years or even longer.

What About Bear Markets?

Some investors believe that while active managers will always have a tough time beating the market when times are good, active managers' market-beating abilities will be revealed during bear markets when lots of negative trends are hurting the market. Stock pickers and market timers, the argument goes, can use their intelligence and insight to sidestep the worst stocks with the poorest prospects or avoid entire asset classes and sectors that stand to get pummeled during a downturn.

---

11 Barras, Laurent, Scaillet ,Wermers, and Russ, "False Discoveries in Mutual Fund Performance: Measuring Luck in Estimated Alphas" (May 2008).

12 Fama, Eugene F. and French, Kenneth R., Luck Versus Skill in the Cross Section of Mutual Fund Returns (December 14, 2009). Tuck School of Business Working Paper No. 2009-56 ; Chicago Booth School of Business Research Paper; Journal of Finance. Available at SSRN: ssrn.com/abstract=1356021.

Unfortunately, for these active managers, the research shows otherwise. For evidence, we only have to look as far back as 2008 — the year of the Great Recession, that saw U.S. stocks (as represented by the S&P 500 Index) plummet 37% in the wake of the worst global financial crisis since the 1930s. That year, actively managed funds as a group underperformed the S&P 500 by an average of 1.67% (see Exhibit 5.3).

Exhibit 5.3: Active Manager Performance During the 2008 Bear Market

Source: Standard and Poor's Investment Service, May 2009. Indexes are not available for direct investment. Their performance does not reflect the expenses associated with the management of an actual portfolio. The data assumes reinvestment of income and does not account for taxes or transaction costs. Past performance is not a guarantee of future results.

Why Has Active Management Failed So Often?

The case against active management is compelling. Yet many investors have a difficult time accepting the facts. It's extremely tempting to think that if we make smart investment decisions — or find a hard-working, brilliant money manager or advisor — we can outperform the market. After all, just because many active managers have struggled to beat the market in the past doesn't mean that someone won't be able to do so in the future, right? If you can find that manager and give him or her all your money today, you'll be rich in no time.

We understand how powerful and motivating that idea can be when making investment decisions. To be honest, there's nothing we'd like better than to find a manager who could beat the market year in and year out for decades and make us fabulously wealthy, too.

The problem with this thinking is that the financial markets operate in ways that make beating them extraordinarily difficult, even for the world's smartest managers. Specifically, there are five challenges that active managers face in trying to outperform the overall market:

Challenge 1: Success Requires Predictive Ability

Wall Street and the popular financial press want you to believe that in order to make money in the stock market, you need to invest based on what's about to happen. That's the message sent out every day by market strategists, brokers, analysts, mutual fund managers and the media — *predict the future accurately, and you'll score big.*

In truth, there is no crystal ball when it comes to investing your money. No one can accurately forecast market movements on a consistent basis. Why? Because we're talking about the future, and the future is by its very nature and definition *unknowable.* We simply cannot know *with certainty* the future direction of the economy, stock prices or the myriad events and developments that will occur that will have an impact on the markets.

Ah, but what about the countless PhDs and other experts on Wall Street who devote their time to sizing up economic and market developments and using their insights to make predictions? Surely they must have an ability to gauge the future that the rest of us lack?

For the answer, consider the following Wall Street predictions for where the S&P 500 would stand on December 31, 2008:

Morgan Stanley 1520
Merrill Lynch 1525
A.G. Edwards 1575
Wachovia Securities 1590
JP Morgan Chase 1590
Bank of America Securities 1625
Goldman Sachs 1675
Citigroup... 1675
Strategas Research Partners.................................. 1680

Actual 2008 S&P 500 Return.................. 903[13]

In other words, none of these highly experienced firms, with access to a wealth of resources and information, were able to foresee an enormous financial panic or predict the down direction of the market that year.

Or take something as seemingly simple as predicting how the broad economy is going to do. As the *New York Times* noted in a May 5, 2009 article, *"Amazingly enough, Wall Street's consensus forecast has failed to predict a single recession in the last 30 years."*[14]

The media's track record is equally abysmal. One of the most famous examples is *Business Week's* August 13, 1979 cover story, *"The Death of Equities."* The article inside reached the conclusion that, *"The death of equities looks like an almost permanent condition — reversible someday, but not soon."* (For the record, the next decade was one of the strongest performing periods for the stock market in history, with the S&P 500 up 17.5% annually.)

For a more recent example, consider this advice from a February 2009 *Forbes* article:

"It's way too early to get back into U.S. stocks…Expect meltdowns in securities backed by credit card debt, home equity, student and auto loans as well as commercial real estate…Avoid emerging markets, especially China."[15]

(For the record, U.S. stocks as measured by the S&P 500 soared 26.5% in 2009, emerging markets as a group shot up 79% and the Chinese market rose 62.6%.)

We could literally fill this book with hundreds of examples of various financial experts and gurus getting it wrong year after year after year. The upshot: Even the brightest analysts, the most famous, highly regarded money managers in the world or the most plugged-in and well-respected financial publications can seldom tell you what's going to happen next, let alone give you reliable advice on how to position your investments to take advantage. That doesn't mean that a fund manager, a talking head on CNBC or the guy who walks his dog down your street every morning won't sometimes get it right. They will. The credit, however, as we've seen, usually goes to luck — not skill. And your financial future is too important to leave to chance.

Challenge 2: The Market Doesn't Give Investors Many Opportunities To Beat It

Every day, there are millions of participants in the stock market. The majority are professional money managers, analysts, strategists and traders with advanced degrees who spend the bulk of their day doing one thing: trying to determine the accurate price of the stocks they're looking to buy and sell. These investors make their judgments by learning all they can about each company: examining corporate documents and financial statements, reading analysts' reports and articles about the firms, listening to conference calls with management, and watching the news for developments about the companies, their suppliers and their competitors as well as the overall economy.

---

13 USA Today. 2008 predictions for the S&P 500. January 2, 2008.

14 www.nytimes.com/2009/05/06/business/economy/06leonhardt

15 www.forbes.com/forbes/2009/0216/106

In other words, all these market participants use all the available information that exists to come up with their opinion of the right price. Investors looking to sell believe the current price is higher than it should be, while potential buyers believe the current price is lower than it should be. As a result, the market participants are constantly negotiating a "fair" price at which they're willing to strike a deal. It's a bit like selling your home and negotiating back and forth with a potential buyer to reach an acceptable price. When both parties agree — a willing seller finds a willing buyer — the transaction closes. Multiply that by millions of transactions every day, and you've got the stock market.

The fact that so many market participants are constantly processing huge amounts of new information to arrive at a fair price means that most stocks are priced efficiently — that is, the price of any stock at any given moment accurately reflects all the known information about it. Whenever any new information comes out, it gets seen and processed by millions of investors at essentially the same time. That causes the price of the stock to almost instantly rise or fall to a new agreed upon "fair" value that once again reflects all the current knowledge about that stock.

As an investor, this means you should generally accept that the price of any stock at a given moment is the price it should be. Why? Because it reflects the collective knowledge of all the investors in the market at that point in time. Naturally, then, the value of the stock market as a whole is accurate at any moment. After all, if those millions of buyers and sellers didn't think prices were fair, no one would ever make a trade. But the fact that more than 8,000 listed stocks change hands every day in the U.S. proves a crucial point: Capital markets are efficient. They allow buyers and sellers to make trades at prices that the participants deem to be fair.

The result of this market efficiency is that the market doesn't easily present any single investor or group of investors with a huge opportunity for outsized profits. Think about it this way: Let's say you are a professional investor with a huge brain and an unflagging work ethic who is trying to beat the market. To do that, you need to uncover opportunities that the other investors don't see. The challenge is, you're surrounded on all sides — on all continents, really — by millions of other extremely smart, incredibly hard-working investors who are also looking to uncover opportunities that go unnoticed. Meanwhile, thanks to technology, all of you are receiving and viewing the same new financial information about companies and the economy at once. Given all that, you would eventually have to ask a key question: What are the chances that you'll see a mistake — a mispricing, in other words — that most or all of your colleagues, peers and competitors won't?

This may hinder a level playing field for individual investors. In the case of a mad dash for the exit, average investors may cash out slower than investors on Wall Street with access to a faster, more efficient high-frequency trading computer. And when the markets recover, a faster computer pipeline will get priority before any average investor through a trading website.

As an investor, all that really matters is where prices land in the longer run, not each day.

Challenge 3: Profiting From Occasional Mispricings Is Tough

That said, just because markets are efficient doesn't mean that market participants are perfectly rational and always make optimal decisions. It's possible that inefficiencies — mispricings — could appear from time to time, as investors' emotions get the best of them and they make judgments about the market based on greed or fear. This concept was most recently evidenced in 2008 and early 2009. Markets plunged, in part because most of the new information that was coming out during that time was extremely negative, but also because much of that new information was unclear and created a huge amount of uncertainty. Investors, left with information that they didn't always know how to process, panicked and drove the market deep into bear territory.

In that environment, an investor might have gone against the herd by aggressively buying stocks when they were severely beaten down — and generated huge gains, when in March 2009 the stock market began to soar. With the benefit of hindsight, you might even claim that any idiot could have seen how mispriced the market was and that stocks were a screaming bargain.

But here's an interesting fact. Although any number of investors could have done exactly those things, they didn't. In fact, they did the exact opposite — they sold stocks and bought bonds. The same fear that prompted investors to sell stocks when times were bleak also stopped them from buying stocks when they were "cheap" and offered the potential for outsized gains. Therefore, the vast majority of investors missed the opportunity to fully participate in the stock market's surprising 2009 surge. The result was — you guessed it — that they missed an amazing opportunity to take part in a tremendous market rally and potentially make a lot of money.

It's not just emotions that make it difficult to take advantage of the occasional mispricing. Once again, think of yourself as that professional investor trying to uncover hidden opportunities. In order to generate a market-beating return, you first need to identify a mistake that everyone else fails to see. But that's just step one. Next, that mistake has to stay around long enough for you to do something about it — another highly unlikely scenario. But let's say that occurs. You "get it right" by buying the stock you identified as mistakenly priced too low by the rest of the world. You're still not done. You have to sell that stock at the right time to a buyer before it dips in value. In other words, to win you have to "get it right" not once, but twice.

Keep in mind that this is just one example. If you or your money manager want to beat the market consistently, you need to make a habit of finding mispricings that last long enough to trade on them and then "get it right twice." Having one great idea isn't going to allow you to beat the market and make you wealthy. You may very well get lucky once or even a few times. But how likely is it that you'll get lucky month after month, year after year for decades? Of course, you already know the answer from Exhibit 5.2: Significantly fewer than one percent of active mutual fund managers had the skill to outperform the broader market over the 32-year period from 1975-2006. As an investor with a lengthy time horizon, you need to honestly assess whether you think you, or your investment managers, fall into that tiny group. Odds are you and your managers won't.

Perhaps you think you can somehow identify the managers who will outperform in the future. Too many investors pick money managers based on past performance. But this is not predictive of future results. Exhibit 5.4 on the following page shows that actively managed funds that achieve top performance in one period typically do not repeat their success in a subsequent period.

Exhibit 5.4: Can Past Performance Predict Future Returns? U.S. Stock Mutual Funds

First Period: January 1998 – December 2007

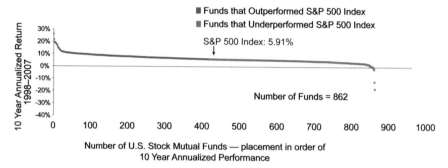

Subsequent Period: January 2008 – December 2012

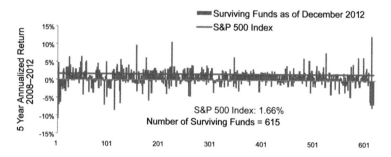

For illustrative purposes only. Mutual funds were placed in descending order of 10-year annualized performance, and subsequent 5-year performance assumes the same ordering as the 10-year period. The number of funds for the subsequent 5-year period represent existing funds from the 10-year period. For the first chart, the eligible universe is all share classes of US Equity Open End mutual funds with a ten-year annualized return as of Dec. 31, 2007, in Morningstar Direct. For the second chart, the eligible universe is all share classes of US Equity Open End mutual funds with a 15-year annualized return as of Dec. 31, 2012, in Morningstar Direct. Sources: Mutual fund universe statistical data provided by Morningstar, Inc.; Indices are not available for direct investment; therefore, their performance does not reflect the expenses associated with the management of an actual portfolio. Past performance is no guarantee of future results, and there is always the risk that an investor may lose money. S&P 500® is a registered trademark of Standard & Poor's Financial Services LLC.

The top graph ranks all U.S. stock mutual funds by their 10-year performance (1998-2007). The bottom graph shows the subsequent five-year performance of these funds (2008-2012). The returns in the bottom graph appear random, illustrating that most mutual fund winners seem unable to maintain their winning streak.

Moreover, 247 funds — or almost 30% — did not even survive and went out of business.

These results are broadly consistent with much of the research into the persistence of mutual fund performance and manager skill. As a whole, this research shows that very, very few managers are able to outperform the markets consistently.

The lesson: Choosing active managers according to past success does not guarantee an equally successful investment outcome in the future.

Challenge 4: The Market's Returns Are Driven By A Select Group Of Stocks That Is Always Changing

You know that stocks overall have delivered positive returns over the long run. What you might not realize is that a relatively small group of stocks has been responsible for that positive return.

For example, looking at the total U.S. stock market database for the period 1926-2012, we find that only the top-performing 25% of stocks were responsible for the market gains during this time frame. The remaining 75% of the stocks collectively generated a loss of -0.6%. (see Exhibit 5.5 on the following page).

Exhibit 5.5: The Impact on Returns of Missing the Top-Performing Stocks (1926 – 2012)

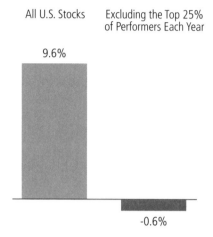

All U.S. Stocks   Excluding the Top 25% of Performers Each Year

9.6%

-0.6%

Source: Results based on the CRSP 1-10 Index. CRSP data provided by the Center for Research in Security Prices, University of Chicago. Past performance is not indicative of future results. Indexes are unmanaged baskets of securities in which investors cannot directly invest. The data assume reinvestment of all dividend and capital gain distributions; they do not include the effect of any taxes, transaction costs or fees charged by an investment advisor or other service provider to an individual account. The risks associated with stocks potentially include increased volatility (up and down movement in the value of your assets) and loss of principal. Small company stocks may be subject to a higher degree of market risk than the securities of more established companies because they tend to be more volatile and less liquid.

The common response from some investors to this statistic is: If a small percentage of stocks could possibly account for the market's long-term returns, why not avoid all the headaches and just invest in these top performing stocks? You know the answer, of course. It's the one written on every prospectus you've ever received: "Past performance is not indicative of future results" — and we know that no one can predict the future with perfect accuracy. A portfolio of even the most carefully screened stocks could easily wind up with none of the best-performing stocks in the market, and thus could possibly produce flat or negative returns over time. As the historical performance of active managers demonstrates, very few of them are accomplished stock pickers. Missing out on even a handful of the top-performing stocks can leave you well short of market returns.

Clearly there is great difficulty and danger inherent in selecting individual stocks. If you had tried to pick winners and avoid losers during the time frame in Exhibit 5.5 you would have put yourself at great risk of not owning the small group of stocks that drove most of the market's return. In essence, you would have been trying to seek out a few needles in an enormous haystack. If you got it right, you did great. If you got it wrong, you did very, very poorly. Either way, the results would have been the same: You would have failed to beat the market.

Conversely, you could have sought out a smart fund manager who you hoped could pick the stocks that would fall into that top 25% category over the long term — or better yet, pick just the best performers from among that select group of winners. But once again, the data tells us that almost no one has been capable of beating the market consistently over long periods of time. By trying to find the tiny handful of managers who might be capable of doing so from among the thousands of professional managers in the business, you'd once again be seeking a small number of needles in a huge haystack.

Challenge 5: Trying To Beat The Market Is Expensive

A final challenge to active management is that returns for active mutual funds may be reduced by higher expenses, since active funds often charge substantial fees and incur heavy trading and tax costs in the efforts to actively move in and out of markets, select specific stocks and "be right twice." In fact, when you look at estimated total fees, including the annual reported net expense ratio and estimated turnover cost, actively managed mutual funds are no bargain. On average, their estimated annual total fees are 1.26% versus 0.67% for passively managed funds — a difference of 0.59% (see Exhibit 5.6).

Exhibit 5.6: Estimated Total Fees for Active vs. Passive Stock Mutual Funds

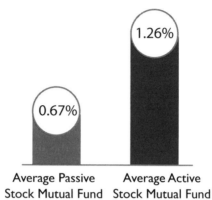

Average Passive   Average Active
Stock Mutual Fund   Stock Mutual Fund

Morningstar Direct April 2013. Passive funds are funds coded as "Index" by Morningstar. Active funds are funds not coded as "Index" by Morningstar. Only distinct U.S. equity open end funds are included. Passive funds exclude leveraged index funds. Annual Report Net Expense Ratio is calculated by taking the average of all the funds' annual report net expense ratios.

The truth is, all those smart and hard-working professionals — the ones who can't seem to beat the market — don't come cheap. In one study, Kenneth R. French, a professor of finance at Dartmouth College's Tuck School of Business, added up the fees and expenses of U.S. stock mutual funds, investment management costs paid by institutions, fees paid to hedge funds and the transaction costs paid by all traders in 2006. Then he deducted what U.S. stock investors would have paid if they had simply bought and held an index fund benchmarked against the overall stock market. The difference between these amounts — the amount that investors pay trying (and failing) to beat the market — was a whopping $102 billion.[16]

A better approach: Accept the market rate of return — it has plenty to offer.

Remember, our goal is to help give you a framework you can utilize to make the smartest possible decisions about your money so you can achieve all that is important to you. One of the smartest decisions you can make is to avoid doing things that history has shown don't work. And the evidence is clear: Trying to beat the market through active management techniques like stock picking and market timing is a real challenge.

The good news is that you don't have to beat the market in order to be a successful investor. Instead, you can take a much smarter, more effective and simpler approach: Own the entire market and stay invested through thick and thin. We saw how missing just a few stocks can diminish your returns. That means the only way you can be assured of owning all of tomorrow's top-performing stocks is to own the entire market all the time.

If you do that, you stand a much better chance of capturing the rate of return that the market has historically generated over time. The less you do to put that positive historical return at risk, the better your chances of coming out ahead in the end.

Here's why: The common goal of all publicly-traded companies is to earn money and maximize the value they provide to their owners — the shareholders. Some of these companies fail to generate earnings and eventually go out of business. Other companies succeed wildly. On balance, more companies have created wealth than destroyed it. We know this because if more companies destroyed wealth than created it, our economy wouldn't grow. Capital markets would have essentially "gone out of business" long ago. But in fact, the exact opposite has occurred.

If you invest your money in shares of publicly-traded companies, you literally own a stake in the wealth that they may create. And as companies create more and more wealth, investors become increasingly willing to pay higher prices to own a piece of that wealth.

This proposition — that you can succeed by joining your fortunes to the future of U.S. and global industry — is hugely powerful. We believe this means that it is prudent and rational to expect stock prices to gradually keep rising over time. We think the stock market should produce a long-

---

16 Kenneth R. French, "The Cost of Active Investing," March 2008.

term positive rate of return because wealth will continue to be created by companies, and stock prices reflect that continual creation of wealth. It means that investing in stocks is not akin to gambling with your money in the hope of making a profit. It is investing in the belief that profits will still be made, that innovation will still occur and that companies will continue to find ways to make money going forward.

That's not to say there won't be blips, speed bumps and the occasional enormous pothole along the way — there most certainly will be. But if you believe in the power of innovation and invest accordingly, you have the opportunity to participate in any rewards and growth that result. The rates of return you may receive as an investor in the entire market will be different for each type of company, depending on the level of risk that is involved in generating its wealth. For example, small firms that are just starting out are generally riskier for investors than large firms that dominate their industries. That's one reason why shares of small publicly traded companies have outperformed shares of the largest firms over time.

Our message is that you shouldn't spend your time and energy trying to pick the right stocks or hunt for the winning manager to achieve your goals. The alternative — investing in assets classes — offers you a simple, straightforward and broadly-diversified approach and frees you from worrying about the ups and downs of individual stocks.

In the end, you will make the choice about how to invest. But given the tremendous challenges of an active management approach, you at least have to ask yourself if it's the most sensible approach to take. If your managers can accomplish the task, you'll be in great shape. If they can't, then you expose yourself and your family to the risk of earning below-market returns.

Is it worth the risk? We believe it isn't.

CHAPTER 6

Risk & Return Are Related

So far we've seen that taking certain types of risks, such as trying to pick winning stocks — and avoiding the losers — and attempting to time markets, have historically failed to generate market-beating returns over the long run. In fact, they may have left many investors with less money than they had originally.

The good news is that there are other types of risk that you may want to consider taking. Markets can be chaotic, but over time they have shown a strong relationship between risk and reward. This means that the compensation for taking on increased levels of risk is the potential to earn greater returns. In fact, when it comes to investing, the return your portfolio earns will be substantially driven by the overall amount of risk you take. But all risks aren't created equal.

According to noted academic research, there are three "factors" or sources of potentially higher returns with higher corresponding risks:[17]

1. Market risk (Stocks vs. Bonds)

2. Size risk (Small Companies vs. Large Companies)

3. Value risk (Value Companies vs. Growth Companies)

---

17 Cross Section of Expected Stock Returns," Eugene F. Fama and Kenneth R. French, Journal of Finance 47 (1992).

These risks were identified and tested by Eugene Fama and Ken French in the early 1990s. Their research resulted in what is known as the Fama-French Three-Factor Model, which has become the basis for portfolio construction for many investors (See Exhibit 6.1). One of the most important jobs for an advisor or investor is to understand the risk factors contained in this model in order to decide how to incorporate them into your portfolio.

Exhibit 6.1: Three-Factor Model

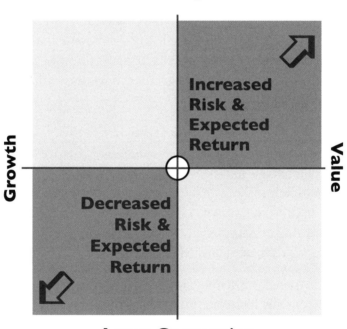

The risks associated with investing in stocks and overweighting small company and value stocks potentially include increased volatility (up and down movement in the value of your assets) and loss of principal.

Risk 1: Market Risk

Market risk is the risk of investing in the stock market versus investing in a "riskless asset," such as a 30-day Treasury bill. Stock investors demand a higher rate of return than investors who buy government bonds in order to compensate them for the increased risk. While past performance is no guarantee of future results, stocks as a whole have outperformed bonds and Treasury bills by a large margin over the last eight decades.[18] As seen in Exhibit 6.2, $1 invested in stocks in 1927 would have grown to $2,996 by the end of 2012 — while that same investment in T-bills would have grown to a mere $20.

Exhibit 6.2: Stocks Outperform Bonds Over Time 1927 – 2012

Source: DFA Returns. DFA Long Term Government Bonds, One Month U.S. Treasury Bills and U.S. Consumer Price Indexes. Fama/French Total U.S. Market Index provided by Fama/French from Center for Research in Security Prices (CRSP) data. Includes all NYSE securities (plus Amex equivalents since July 1962 and NASDAQ equivalents since 1973), including utilities. Risks associated with investing in stocks potentially include increased volatility (up and down movement in the value of your assets) and loss of principal. Indexes are unmanaged baskets of securities that investors cannot directly invest in. Past performance is no guarantee of future results. Hypothetical value of $1 invested at the beginning of 1927 and kept invested through December 31, 2012. Assumes reinvestment of income and no transaction costs or taxes. This is for illustrative purposes only and not indicative of any investment. An investment cannot be made directly in an index.

---

18 Represented by the Fama/French Total U.S. Market Index, which consists of all the securities listed on the New York Stock Exchange plus American Stock Exchange equivalents since July 1962 and NASDAQ equivalents since 1973.

The relationship between risk and return makes sense. Investors can buy a short-term Treasury bill, which is essentially a loan to the U.S. government, and take minimal risk. Or they can invest in the broad stock market — in other words, own a piece of the current and future profits of many companies. As a partial owner of public companies, you accept more risk than if you are simply a lender to the government — and you should expect a greater return because of your willingness to accept that additional risk.

This relationship also extends to bonds issued by corporations. If a company declares bankruptcy, its bondholders may be able to recover some or all of their original investment. Stockholders have less likelihood of recovering their investment, as their claims are subordinate to those of bondholders. Because of additional risk, stockholders have tended to demand a higher return than bondholders.

Investing in the stock market carries risk that doesn't always reward investors year in and year out. There have been long periods when bonds outperformed stocks. For example, the 10-year period through 2012 saw the S&P 500 Index return 7.1% annually while the Bank of America Merrill Lynch 1-3 Year Treasury/Agency Index gained 2.8%.

The good news, however, is long-term historical averages indicate that investors have been compensated over the long term for their willingness to take on market risk.

Risk 2: Size Risk

One common way stocks are categorized is by by size. Large-company stocks are shares of firms with large market capitalizations (defined as the stock's price per share multiplied by the number of shares outstanding), while small-company stocks have small market capitalizations. A large company might be a multi-national firm with tens of thousands of employees. A small firm could have just a few hundred or even several dozen employees.

In Exhibit 6.3, you can see that historically, small-company stocks have grown an average of 11.5%, versus 9.6% for large-company stocks. A dollar invested in 1927 in U.S. Small Cap would be worth $12,013 at the end of 2012, versus $2,548 for U.S. Large Cap.

Exhibit 6.3: Small-Caps Outperform Large-Caps Over Time
Monthly: January 1927 – December 2012

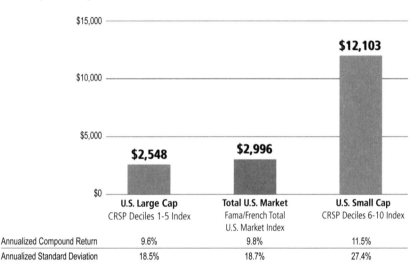

	U.S. Large Cap CRSP Deciles 1-5 Index	Total U.S. Market Fama/French Total U.S. Market Index	U.S. Small Cap CRSP Deciles 6-10 Index
Annualized Compound Return	9.6%	9.8%	11.5%
Annualized Standard Deviation	18.5%	18.7%	27.4%

Source: DFA Returns. Fama/French Total U.S. Market Index provided by Fama/French from Center for Research in Security Prices (CRSP) data. Includes all NYSE securities (plus Amex equivalents since July 1962 and NASDAQ equivalents since 1973), including utilities. The Center for Research in Security Prices (CRSP) ranks all NYSE companies by market capitalization and divides them into 10 equally-populated portfolios. AMEX and NASDAQ National Market stocks are then placed into deciles according to their respective capitalizations, determined by the NYSE breakpoints. CRSP 1-5 Index represents large caps and 6-10 Index represents small caps. Small company stocks may be subject to a higher degree of market risk than the securities of more established companies because they may be more volatile and less liquid. Standard deviation is a statistical measurement of how far the return of a security (or index) moves above or below its average value. The greater the standard deviation, the riskier an investment is considered to be. Indexes are unmanaged baskets of securities that investors cannot directly invest in. Past performance is no guarantee of future results. Hypothetical value of $1 invested at the beginning of 1927 and kept invested through December 31, 2012. Assumes reinvestment of income and no transaction costs or taxes. This is for illustrative purposes only and not indicative of any investment. Total returns in U.S. dollars.

Why is this the case?

Simple: Small-company stocks are riskier than large company stocks. Smaller firms typically are younger and less financially stable than their larger, older peers. They also tend to have less stable or consistent earnings from year to year than the largest, most established firms so they are less able to withstand economic downturns. For example, compare Starbucks with a hypothetical smaller, upstart competitor we'll call for the sake of this example New Brews.

Smaller firms (like New Brews) have the potential to grow into giants (like Starbucks). But they also are more likely to go out of business if they experience problems; their smaller size and capital base mean they have a smaller financial cushion to help them weather a downturn in business conditions. Because of these risks, investors demand a higher return when they buy shares of small companies. The risk that Starbucks will implode is relatively low. After all, they're on practically every street corner in America — and around the world. As a result, investors in Starbucks are willing to accept a relatively low return on their investment. However, the risk that New Brews will implode is significantly higher. Investors will only buy shares in New Brews if they can reasonably expect to earn a higher return to compensate them for incurring additional risk. In short, if New Brews didn't offer a higher potential return, do you think any investors would choose them over Starbucks?

Small-company stocks do not always outperform large-company stocks. In fact, many years can go by during which this size premium reverses and shares of larger firms beat shares of smaller companies — sometimes by very significant margins. However, as you can see from Exhibit 6.4, small-company stocks have historically outperformed their larger peers over time. In fact, small stocks beat large stocks 84% of the time over rolling 20-year periods from July 1926 to 2012, and 95% of the time over rolling 25-year periods. (Rolling returns are the annualized average return for a period ending with the listed year.)

Exhibit 6.4: U.S. Small Stocks vs. U.S. Large Stocks
July 1926 – 2012

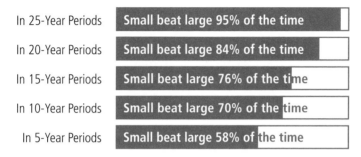

In 25-Year Periods	Small beat large 95% of the time
In 20-Year Periods	Small beat large 84% of the time
In 15-Year Periods	Small beat large 76% of the time
In 10-Year Periods	Small beat large 70% of the time
In 5-Year Periods	Small beat large 58% of the time

Periods based on rolling annualized returns. 745 total 25-year periods. 805 total 20-year periods. 865 total 15-year periods. 925 total 10-year periods. 985 total 5-year periods.

Source: DFA Returns. The Center for Research in Security Prices (CRSP) ranks all NYSE companies by market capitalization and divides them into 10 equally-populated portfolios. AMEX and NASDAQ National Market stocks are then placed into deciles according to their respective capitalizations, determined by the NYSE breakpoints. CRSP 1-5 Index represents large caps and 6-10 Index represents small caps. Small company stocks may be subject to a higher degree of market risk than the securities of more established companies because they may be more volatile and less liquid. Indexes are unmanaged baskets of securities that investors cannot directly invest in. Past performance is no guarantee of future results. Assumes reinvestment of income and no transaction costs or taxes. This is for illustrative purposes only and not indicative of any investment. An investment cannot be made directly in an index.

Risk 3: Value Risk

The third type of risk identified by Fama and French's research pertains to growth stocks versus value stocks.

Value stocks are usually associated with corporations that have experienced slower earnings growth or sales, or have recently experienced business difficulties, causing their stock prices to fall. These value companies are often regarded as turnaround opportunities, where a change in management, strategy or other factors could improve the company's prospects and its earnings.

Historically, the earning streams of value stocks have been much more uncertain than growth stocks. This means the market has to assign them lower prices in order to attract investors.

Though they are riskier than growth companies, emphasizing value companies in a portfolio may lead to both increased diversification and the expectation of potentially higher returns.

In Exhibit 6.5, you can see that historically, large value has grown an average of 10.2% per year, versus 9.1% annually for large growth. A dollar invested in 1927 in large value would be worth $4,336 at the end of 2012, versus $1,805 for large growth.

Exhibit 6.5: U.S. Value Outperforms U.S. Growth Over Time
Growth of $1 January 1, 1927 – December 31, 2012

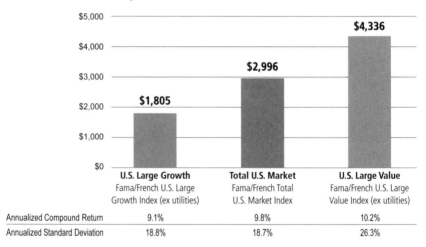

	U.S. Large Growth Fama/French U.S. Large Growth Index (ex utilities)	Total U.S. Market Fama/French Total U.S. Market Index	U.S. Large Value Fama/French U.S. Large Value Index (ex utilities)
Annualized Compound Return	9.1%	9.8%	10.2%
Annualized Standard Deviation	18.8%	18.7%	26.3%

Source: DFA Returns. CRSP is the Center for Research in Security Prices. CRSP ranks all NYSE companies by market capitalization and divides them into 10 equally-populated portfolios. AMEX and NASDAQ National Market stocks are then placed into deciles according to their respective capitalizations, determined by the NYSE breakpoints. Value is represented by companies with a book-to-market ratio in the top 30% of all companies. Growth is represented by companies with a book-to-market ratio in the bottom 30% of all companies. The CRSP Value and Growth divisions within the CRSP 1-5 Portfolios are employed to formulate the Fama/French U.S Large Value Index and Fama/French U.S Large Growth Index. Fama/French Total U.S. Market Index provided by Fama/French from Center for Research in Security Prices (CRSP) data. Includes all NYSE securities (plus Amex equivalents since July 1962 and NASDAQ equivalents since 1973), including utilities. Fama/French U.S. Large Growth Index provided by Fama/French from Center for Research in Security Prices (CRSP) data. Includes the upper-half range in market cap and the lower 30% in book-to-market of NYSE securities (plus Amex equivalents since July 1962 and NASDAQ equivalents since 1973), excluding utilities. Fama/French U.S. Large Value Index provided by Fama/French from CRSP data. Includes the upper-half range in market cap and the higher 30% in book-to-market of NYSE securities (plus Amex equivalents since July 1962 and NASDAQ equivalents since 1973), excluding utilities. The risks associated with investing in value stocks potentially include increased volatility (up and down movement in the value of your assets) and loss of principal. Standard deviation is a statistical measurement of how far the return of a security (or index) moves above or below its average value. The greater the standard deviation, the riskier an investment is considered to be. Indexes are unmanaged baskets of securities that investors cannot directly invest in. Past performance is no guarantee of future results. Hypothetical value of $1 invested at the beginning of 1927 and kept invested through December 31, 2012. Assumes reinvestment of income and no transaction costs or taxes. This is for illustrative purposes only and not indicative of any investment. Total returns in U.S. dollars.

In Exhibit 6.6, you can see how value has fared versus growth over various time periods. Value stocks have historically outperformed growth stocks over time. In fact, value stocks beat growth stocks 84% of the time over rolling 20-year periods from July 1926 to 2012, and 91% of the time over rolling 25-year periods. (Rolling returns are the annualized average return for a period ending with the listed year.)

Exhibit 6.6: U.S. Value vs. U.S. Growth
July 1926 – December 2012

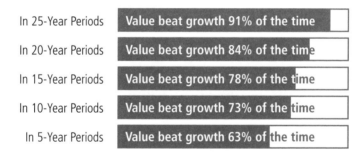

Periods based on rolling annualized returns. 727 total 25-year periods. 787 total 20-year periods. 847 total 15-year periods. 907 total 10-year periods. 967 total 5-year periods.

Source: DFA Returns. CRSP is the Center for Research in Security Prices. CRSP ranks all NYSE companies by market capitalization and divides them into 10 equally-populated portfolios. AMEX and NASDAQ National Market stocks are then placed into deciles according to their respective capitalizations, determined by the NYSE breakpoints. Value is represented by companies with a book-to-market ratio in the top 30% of all companies. Growth is represented by companies with a book-to-market ratio in the bottom 30% of all companies. The CRSP Value and Growth divisions within the CRSP 1-5 Portfolios are employed to formulate the Fama/French U.S. Large Value Index and Fama/French U.S. Large Growth Index. Includes all NYSE securities (plus Amex equivalents since July 1962 and NASDAQ equivalents since 1973), including utilities. Fama/French U.S. Large

Growth Index provided by Fama/French from Center for Research in Security Prices (CRSP) data. Includes the upper-half range in market cap and the lower 30% in book-to-market of NYSE securities (plus Amex equivalents since July 1962 and NASDAQ equivalents since 1973), excluding utilities. Fama/French U.S. Large Value Index provided by Fama/French from CRSP data. Includes the upper-half range in market cap and the higher 30% in book-to-market of NYSE securities (plus Amex equivalents since July 1962 and NASDAQ equivalents since 1973), excluding utilities. The risks associated with investing in value stocks potentially include increased volatility (up and down movement in the value of your assets) and loss of principal. Indexes are unmanaged baskets of securities that investors cannot directly invest in. Past performance is no guarantee of future results. Assumes reinvestment of income and no transaction costs or taxes. This is for illustrative purposes only and not indicative of any investment.

Here again risk drives reward. In this case, consider the characteristics of value stocks: They are out of favor with investors, who see such firms as risky — especially when compared to growth companies, which are usually characterized by strong earnings growth and high returns on equity.

In order to allocate investment capital to value stocks, investors demand greater compensation than they do from the more stable growth companies. If these value stocks didn't offer higher expected returns, and correspondingly reflect higher prices as assigned by the market, no one would bother investing in them.

As an example, consider two well-known retailers: Sears and Walmart. In recent years Sears has encountered numerous hurdles that caused its sales to significantly lag its competitors. In fact, Sears was actually bought by Kmart — the discount retailer that was in such bad financial shape in 2002 that it declared bankruptcy. By contrast, Walmart experienced strong growth in sales and profits during the past decade and by many metrics would have to be considered superior to Sears (and Kmart).

And yet, as seen in Exhibit 6.7, Sears stock has delivered much higher returns than Walmart stock during the past seven years or so. While Sears stock soared as high as 1200% during that time, Walmart stock was essentially flat. How can that possibly be the case? It's because Sears was a riskier investment than "sure-thing" Walmart. Notice how volatile Sears' stock returns are compared to Walmart's; that extra risk compensated investors with a much higher return.

Exhibit 6.7: Sears Stock vs. Walmart Stock
May 2, 2003 – December 31, 2012

Source: Loring Ward; Yahoo Finance. This is for illustrative purposes only. This type of value vs. growth phenomena is not always the case. Value companies will not always outperform growth companies, and there have been historical periods when growth has significantly outpaced value.

Still, this idea that value stocks are riskier than growth stocks is hard for some investors to grasp. Many investors assume the opposite — that because innovative growth companies take bigger chances than distressed value companies they're riskier and therefore more likely to reward investors.

On first blush, this sounds reasonable. But remember that value stocks are stocks with low relative prices. Why? Because investors have pushed down value stocks' prices to compensate for all that risk. Value stocks have more earnings uncertainty than growth stocks, for example. In the face of this type of uncertainty, investors often sell value stocks, driving their prices lower. Then, as many of these distressed companies solve their financial problems and become healthier, investors start to pay attention, buy the shares and drive up the prices. So even though it might sound a little strange, the "bad" value companies perform better as an investment than the "good" growth companies over the long run.

The small and value risk premiums that have been historically evident in the U.S. have been even more persistent in the international markets given the data that is available. As you can see from Exhibit 6.8, in the international markets, value stocks and small company stocks have outperformed the commonly used broad international index. The value premium has been especially strong and even more persistent than the size premium in the international markets.

EXHIBIT 6.8: International Value vs. International Growth and International Small vs. International Large

Overlapping Periods	Jan. 1975 – Dec. 2012 International Value vs. International Growth	Jan. 1970 – Dec. 2012 International Small vs. International Large
In 25-Year Periods	Value beat growth 100% of the time	Small beat large 100% of the time
In 20-Year Periods	Value beat growth 100% of the time	Small beat large 97% of the time
In 15-Year Periods	Value beat growth 100% of the time	Small beat large 83% of the time
In 10-Year Periods	Value beat growth 100% of the time	Small beat large 80% of the time
In 5-Year Periods	Value beat growth 98% of the time	Small beat large 79% of the time

Based on rolling annualized returns. Rolling multi-year periods overlap and are not independent. This statistical dependence must be considered when assessing the reliability of long-horizon return differences. International Value vs. International Growth data: 145 overlapping 25-year periods. 205 overlapping 20-year periods. 265 overlapping 15-year periods. 325 overlapping 10-year periods. 385 overlapping 5-year periods. International Small vs. International Large data: 205 overlapping 25-year periods. 265 overlapping 20-year periods. 325 overlapping 15-year periods. 385 overlapping 10-year periods. 445 overlapping 5-year periods. Source: DFA Returns. International Value represented by Fama/French International Value Index. International Growth represented by Fama/French International Growth Index. International Small represented by Dimensional International Small Cap Index. International Large represented by MSCI World ex USA Index (gross div.). All investments involve risk. Foreign securities involve additional risks including foreign currency changes, taxes and different accounting and financial reporting methods. Small company stocks may be subject to a higher degree of market risk than the securities of more established companies because they may be more volatile and less liquid. The risks associated with investing in value stocks potentially include increased volatility (up and down movement in the value of your assets) and loss of principal. Indexes are unmanaged baskets of securities that investors cannot directly invest in. Past performance is no guarantee of future results. Assumes reinvestment of income and no transaction costs or taxes. This is for illustrative purposes only and not indicative of any investment.

What Do The Market, Size And Value Premiums Mean For Investors

The data in this chapter, culled from decades of research, is intended to help investors understand the risks that may generate returns. Research on financial markets is ongoing, and our knowledge will continue to expand. But what we do know about risk and return provide a framework for building and maintaining your portfolio. Your job doesn't need to be focused on picking the right stocks and avoiding the wrong ones.

Instead, we believe your investment strategy should center around a couple of major decisions. First, decide how much overall market risk you want, and are able, to take. That decision will impact how much money is allocated to stocks versus bonds, T-bills and cash. Then, within the stock portion of your portfolio, how much small and value risk are you willing to take on to potentially enhance returns?

If you want, and are able, to take on more risk in pursuit of higher expected returns, you can increase your exposure to small-company stocks, value stocks or both. If you're more concerned about safety and stability, you can increase your exposure to bonds.

In the next chapter, we'll discuss specific diversification strategies that will help you keep your wealth management plan on track regardless of what the markets are doing.

CHAPTER 7

Effective Diversification

The third component of successful investing is diversifying your portfolio across multiple types of assets and investments. Effective diversification enables investors to potentially reduce the overall risk in their portfolios and increase their portfolios' long-term potential returns.

Diversification is a well-known term, of course. But far too many investors still don't fully understand what it really means or even why they should take the time to build and maintain well-diversified portfolios. Even if you think you know all there is to know about diversification, we urge you to read this chapter so you can determine if your efforts at diversification are truly on target or if you need to reevaluate your approach. Diversification can be employed at multiple levels to increase its effectiveness.

The Case for Diversification

Investors sometimes question the need for diversification. Instead of allocating their wealth by investing in a wide range of assets, investment styles, and markets, they ask, "Why not just put all my money in investments that have a history of beating other assets and the overall market?"

The reason, as anyone who lost sleep during the market meltdown of the "Great Recession" can tell you, is that no single type of asset always performs well. It's true that stocks, as measured by the Fama/French Total U.S. Market Index, have performed well over the long term, gaining 9.8% annually from 1927-2012.[19] But that long-term return was

---

19 Fama/French Total U.S. Market Index provided by Fama/French from Center for Research in Security Prices (CRSP) data. Includes all NYSE securities (plus Amex equivalents since July 1962 and NASDAQ equivalents since 1973), including utilities.

of little comfort during the 2008 bear market when the S&P 500 index plummeted nearly 40%.

But remember: Investing is all about the future — what's going to happen. In order for you to successfully shift your money from one investment to the next, you would have to know what stock, sector or asset class is going to outperform the others going forward. And the future is, by its very nature, unknowable — none of us can be completely certain what is going to occur in the next five minutes, five days or five years. There will always be unanticipated events that affect the world and, therefore, your investments.

For example, ask yourself if you've ever had an investment that didn't work out. Why didn't it perform as planned? Because you (or the person managing your money) didn't anticipate a development that affected your investment. Every active money manager wants to beat the market, yet so few actually do. We believe that no one — not even the brightest minds on Wall Street — can accurately predict the future time and time again. If they could, they'd beat the market year after year after year. As you saw in Chapter 5, that just hasn't happened.

The upshot: It's nearly impossible to know when an asset class will outperform and when it will fall to the bottom of the pack. Indeed, the asset class that wins the performance race in one year rarely is capable of defending its crown the next — and a losing asset class one year often unexpectedly soars to the top of the list the next year. As you can see from Exhibit 7.1, in 1999, emerging markets shares soared almost 66% and were the top-performing stock category for the year. The worst category that year was REITs (Real Estate Investment Trusts), which fell 5%. But in the very next year, emerging markets fell to the bottom of the pack, declining 30%. The top performing category of 2000 was REITs, up 26%.

Exhibit 7.1: Asset Class Index Performance 1998 – 2012

High ↑ (top rows) → Low ↓ (bottom rows)

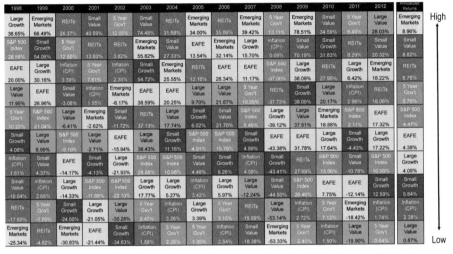

Rank	1998	1999	2000	2001	2002	2003	2004	2005	2006	2007	2008	2009	2010	2011	2012	Annualized Returns
1 (High)	Large Growth 36.65%	Emerging Markets 66.49%	REITs 26.37%	Small Value 40.59%	5 Year Gov't 12.95%	Small Value 74.48%	REITs 31.58%	Emerging Markets 34.00%	REITs 35.06%	Emerging Markets 39.42%	5 Year Gov't 13.11%	Emerging Markets 78.51%	Small Value 34.59%	5 Year Gov't 9.46%	Large Value 28.03%	Emerging Markets 8.96%
2	S&P 500 Index 28.58%	Small Growth 54.06%	5 Year Gov't 12.80%	REITs 13.93%	REITs 3.82%	Emerging Markets 55.82%	Small Value 27.33%	EAFE 13.54%	Emerging Markets 32.14%	Large Growth 15.70%	Inflation (CPI) 0.09%	Small Value 70.19%	Small Growth 31.83%	REITs 8.29%	Small Value 20.32%	Small Value 8.82%
3	EAFE 20.00%	Large Growth 30.16%	Inflation (CPI) 3.39%	5 Year Gov't 7.61%	Inflation (CPI) 2.38%	Small Growth 54.72%	Emerging Markets 25.55%	REITs 12.16%	EAFE 26.34%	EAFE 11.17%	S&P 500 Index -37.00%	Large Growth 38.09%	REITs 27.96%	Large Growth 6.42%	Emerging Markets 18.22%	REITs 8.78%
4	Large Value 11.95%	EAFE 26.96%	Small Value -3.08%	Inflation (CPI) 1.55%	Emerging Markets -6.17%	EAFE 38.59%	EAFE 20.25%	Large Value 9.70%	Large Value 21.87%	5 Year Gov't 10.05%	REITs -37.73%	Small Growth 38.06%	Large Value 20.17%	Inflation (CPI) 2.96%	REITs 18.06%	5 Year Gov't 5.79%
5	5 Year Gov't 10.22%	S&P 500 Index 21.04%	Large Value -6.41%	Emerging Markets -2.62%	Small Value -11.72%	REITs 37.13%	Large Value 17.74%	Small Growth 6.02%	Small Value 21.70%	S&P 500 Index 5.49%	Large Growth -39.12%	EAFE 31.78%	Emerging Markets 18.88%	S&P 500 Index 2.11%	EAFE 17.32%	S&P 500 Index 4.47%
6	Small Growth 4.08%	Large Value 6.99%	S&P 500 Index -9.10%	Large Value -2.71%	EAFE -15.94%	Large Value 36.43%	Small Growth 17.77%	S&P 500 Index 4.91%	S&P 500 Index 15.79%	Small Growth 4.99%	Small Growth -43.38%	Large Value 31.51%	Large Growth 17.64%	Small Value -4.43%	Large Growth 17.22%	EAFE 4.38%
7	Inflation (CPI) 1.61%	Small Value 4.37%	EAFE -14.17%	S&P 500 Index -11.89%	Large Value -21.93%	S&P 500 Index 28.68%	S&P 500 Index 10.88%	Small Value 4.46%	Small Growth 11.16%	Inflation (CPI) 4.08%	Large Value -43.41%	REITs 27.99%	S&P 500 Index 15.06%	EAFE -10.78%	S&P 500 Index 16.00%	Large Growth 4.08%
8	Small Value -10.04%	Inflation (CPI) 2.68%	Large Growth -14.33%	Large Growth -20.28%	S&P 500 Index -22.10%	Large Growth 25.90%	Large Growth 5.27%	Inflation (CPI) 3.42%	Large Growth 9.26%	Large Value -12.24%	Small Value -44.50%	S&P 500 Index 26.46%	EAFE 7.75%	Large Value -12.14%	Small Growth 12.59%	Small Growth 3.84%
9	REITs -17.50%	5 Year Gov't -1.76%	Small Growth -24.50%	Small Growth -21.05%	Large Growth -30.28%	5 Year Gov't 2.40%	Inflation (CPI) 3.26%	Large Growth 2.54%	5 Year Gov't 4.08%	REITs -15.69%	EAFE -53.14%	Inflation (CPI) 2.72%	5 Year Gov't 7.12%	Emerging Markets -18.42%	Inflation (CPI) 1.74%	Inflation (CPI) 2.38%
10 (Low)	Emerging Markets -25.34%	REITs -4.62%	Emerging Markets -30.83%	EAFE -21.44%	Small Growth -34.63%	Inflation (CPI) 1.88%	5 Year Gov't 2.26%	5 Year Gov't 1.35%	Inflation (CPI) 2.54%	Small Value -18.38%	Emerging Markets -53.33%	5 Year Gov't -2.40%	Inflation (CPI) 1.50%	Small Growth -19.90%	5 Year Gov't 0.64%	Large Value 0.87%

Data Sources: DFA Returns, Morningstar Direct. All investments involve risk. Foreign securities involve additional risks, including foreign currency changes, political risks, foreign taxes, and different methods of accounting and financial reporting. Past performance is not indicative of future performance. Treasury bills are guaranteed as to repayment of principal and interest by the U.S. government. This information does not constitute a solicitation for sale of any securities. CRSP ranks all NYSE companies by market capitalization and divides them into 10 equally-populated portfolios. AMEX and NASDAQ National Market stocks are then placed into deciles according to their respective capitalizations, determined by the NYSE breakpoints. CRSP Portfolios 1-5 represent large-cap stocks; Portfolios 6-10 represent small-caps; Value is represented by companies with a book-to-market ratio in the top 30% of all companies. Growth is represented by companies with a book-to-market ratio in the bottom 30% of all companies. S&P 500 Index is the Standard & Poor's 500 Index. The S&P 500 Index measures the performance of large-capitalization U.S. stocks. The S&P 500 is an unmanaged market value-weighted index of 500 stocks that are traded on the NYSE, AMEX and NASDAQ. The weightings make each company's influence on the index performance directly proportional to that company's market value. S&P 500® is a registered trademark of Standard & Poor's Financial Services LLC. The MSCI EAFE Index (Morgan Stanley Capital International Europe, Australasia, Far East Index) is comprised of over 1,000 companies representing the stock markets of Europe, Australia, New Zealand and the Far East, and is an unmanaged index. EAFE represents non-U.S. large stocks. Consumer Price Index (CPI) is a measure of inflation. REITs, represented by the NAREIT Equity REIT Index, is an unmanaged market cap-weighted index comprised of 151 equity REITS. Emerging Markets index represents securities in countries with developing economies and provide potentially high returns. Many Latin American, Eastern European and Asian countries are considered emerging markets. Indexes are unmanaged baskets of securities without the fees and expenses associated with mutual funds and other investments. Investors cannot directly invest in an index.

Based on historical stock market information, returns appear random in the short term. So if you want to own winning assets each year, you can't just invest in one or two asset class categories. Instead, you need to own a variety in order to avoid concentration in any one in particular. Some of these asset classes may be performing well at a given time, while others will be lagging. That's how diversification works.

During the financial crisis and market meltdown of 2008, if you had been invested in just one asset class, such as the S&P 500, your net worth may have been down about 37%. However, if you diversified and built a portfolio that included bonds and cash, asset classes which both experienced positive returns in 2008, you would have been in better shape.

In fact, the benefits of diversification are often most evident during bear markets. Exhibit 7.2 illustrates the growth of stocks versus a diversified portfolio during two of the worst performance periods in recent history.

The blue line illustrates the hypothetical growth of $1,000 invested in stocks during the mid-1970s recession and the Great Recession of 2007–2011. The green line illustrates the hypothetical growth of $1,000 invested in a diversified portfolio of 35% stocks, 40% bonds, and 25% Treasury bills during these same two periods.

Over the course of both time periods, the diversified portfolio lost less than the pure stock portfolio.

Exhibit 7.2: Performance of Diversified Portfolios vs. Pure Stock Portfolios During & After Bear Markets

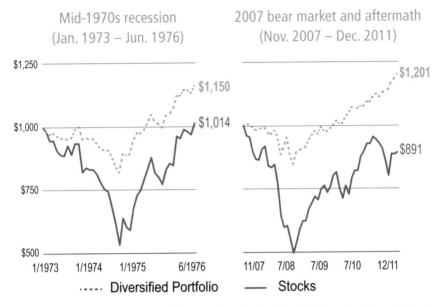

Mid-1970s recession
(Jan. 1973 – Jun. 1976)

2007 bear market and aftermath
(Nov. 2007 – Dec. 2011)

····· Diversified Portfolio —— Stocks

Past performance is no guarantee of future results. Diversified portfolio: 35% stocks, 40% bonds, 25% Treasury bills. Hypothetical value of $1,000 invested at the beginning of January 1973 and November 2007, respectively. This is for illustrative purposes only and not indicative of any investment. An investment cannot be made directly in an index. Stocks in this example are represented by the S&P 500, bonds are represented by the 20-year U.S. Government Bond, and Treasury bills by the 30-day U.S. Treasury bill. The data assumes reinvestment of income and does not account for taxes or transaction costs. ©2012 Morningstar.

Think about the potential benefits of diversification this way. Say you're packing to go on an extensive road trip across the country. Along the way you plan to hit some Florida beaches, so you pack sunscreen. You also will visit relatives in New England, so you pack some sweaters in case it's cold. In addition, your travels will take you to the Pacific Northwest, so you make sure to include an umbrella. By being prepared for the wide variety of conditions you're likely to experience during your long trip, you'll reduce the risk of having negative moments and maximize your probability of enjoying your experiences no matter where you are along the way.

Diversification is the key to packing wisely for an investment journey. It helps make you better prepared to deal with the various experiences you'll have along the way.

It is important to make a distinction here between two types of risk, as shown in Exhibit 7.3. "Systematic risk" (also known as market risk) cannot be minimized or eliminated through diversification — in other words, if you invest in stocks, you must be willing to accept market risk. On the other hand, "unsystematic risk" — the risk that's inherent in investing in a single company or even a group of companies in a single industry — can be diminished by diversification.

Exhibit 7.3: Systematic and Unsystematic Risks

Total Stock Risk

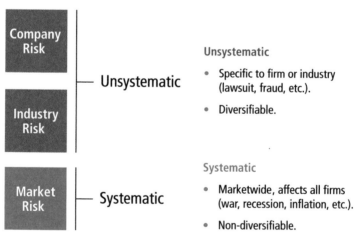

If your portfolio consists entirely of one stock — a financial services company, for example — your level of wealth is dependent entirely on the value of that stock. If the company experiences a significant setback or goes out of business, your wealth can be destroyed. Consider, for example, if all or even the majority of your portfolio were invested in Lehman Brothers stock or Wachovia or GM or AIG or any of the other companies that ran into severe troubles during the "Great Recession."

But adding another stock to that portfolio immediately reduces the risk that a blow-up at the first company will destroy your wealth. If that second stock is from an entirely different industry (i.e. technology) whose health and stability are affected by different factors, that risk may fall even further. If you then add a third stock from an entirely different area of the market (i.e. an oil company in a small overseas market) you cut your risk further still. Repeat this process thousands of times and you have the basis for a diversified stock portfolio in which no single company, industry or country has a disproportionate ability to damage your wealth. Then by adding other types of assets beyond stocks — such as bonds — you can further enhance your diversification and further decrease your risk.

The end result: The losses you'll experience when some investment assets perform poorly may be offset by gains from other investment assets that are doing well.

This approach is what we refer to as effective diversification — building a broadly diversified portfolio that tries to maximize return for your chosen level of risk.

If you own many different asset classes and many different individual investments within those asset classes, you don't have to worry as much if one or even many of those investments don't pan out — you have a whole host of other investments to help make up for the losers. And your portfolio likely won't experience the extreme, nerve-wracking swings in value that a highly concentrated portfolio would. The less worried you are about your portfolio and the less volatile it is from year to year, the less likely you'll be to panic during market downturns and make poor decisions — like selling out of stocks right at a market bottom — that could damage your financial future.

There's another potential benefit to diversification that is just as powerful yet less appreciated: Lowering volatility has a potential impact on the growth of wealth over time.

For illustration purposes only, consider exhibit 7.4 below, which shows two $100,000 portfolios. Each one has an average monthly return of 1%. But note that Investment A's return each month swings dramatically between +10% and -8%. By contrast, Investment B is much less volatile. Its monthly return alternates between just +4% and -2%. Even though both investments produce the same monthly return, the lower volatility of Investment B generates much more growth over time. An investor in volatile Investment A would have ended up with much less wealth over three decades — some $2.2 million less, in fact. In stark contrast, an investor in the less volatile Investment B would have done a much better job protecting and growing his or her wealth.

Exhibit 7.4: The Potential Impact of Volatility on a $100,000 Portfolio

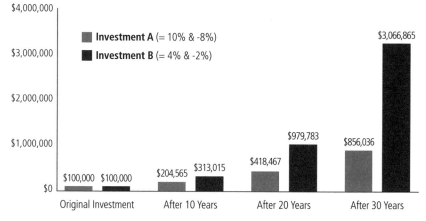

Source: Loring Ward. For illustrative purposes only. Each investment has an average monthly return of 1%, but very different volatility profiles. Investment A (higher volatility) achieves the 1% return by alternating monthly between 10% and –8%, while Investment B (lower volatility) achieves the same average return by alternating between 4% and –2%. The table shows the value of an initial investment of $100,000 with no additions or withdrawals invested over 10, 20 and 30 years. Investments A and B are not representative of a real investment, i.e., no dividends are paid and there are no management fees deducted.

The reason volatility can hamper growth? Significant losses reduce the principal value of the investment portfolio which essentially reduces the base upon which further gains may be earned. For example, if an investor loses 50% on a $1 million portfolio, the new principal base is only $500,000. The investor will need to double his money simply to recover the loss. The bigger the loss, the longer the recovery period.

Is Diversification On The Ropes?

It's important to recognize that while effective diversification can help reduce a portfolio's overall volatility and increase its potential returns, it cannot guarantee that you won't lose money. This is especially true when there are huge shocks to global markets and economies — such as the worldwide credit crisis that resulted from the blow-up in subprime mortgages in 2008. The depth and breadth of these problems shook the global financial system to its core and left investors with very few places to hide.

In that environment, asset classes that would normally react differently to an event tended to move together. For example, most major stock categories — large stocks, small stocks, large foreign shares and emerging markets stocks — all fell by 30% or more. Holding a mix of various types of stocks did investors little good that year — a situation that prompted some investors and investment gurus to declare that diversification was dead.

However, we believe that diversification is as alive and well as ever. One common misconception about diversification is that as one market or asset class goes down, another invariably goes up — for example, when the U.S. market falls, overseas markets rise. Such an offset is more than we can reasonably expect from diversification.

We spoke earlier about systematic and unsystematic risk — which represents the specific risks associated with an investment asset, whether it be default risk or earnings risk for a specific stock or political and currency risk for a particular country. Unsystematic risk can be diminished by combining many different countries so that the risk and returns may offset one another, thereby smoothing the potential return of the portfolio.

During periods of global market crisis, market risk dominates any other specific risk factor for an individual investment. For this reason, all assets may decline simultaneously. However, this does not imply that there are no benefits to diversification during this period.

To see why, it's necessary to understand the concept of correlation which is simply how similar or dissimilar the pattern of returns of one asset class corresponds with another asset class. If two asset classes have a positive correlation, their values will move simultaneously in the same direction. If the two asset classes have a negative correlation, their prices will move in opposite directions. Combining asset classes with negative correlations can give your portfolio a smoother ride over time. By contrast, owning various asset classes with positive correlations gives you less overall diversification.

Many people assume that the correlation between different asset classes is completely negative and that their prices move in opposite directions. In fact, nearly all correlations between investments are positive to some degree, but the magnitude of the gains and losses will be different. Indeed, that's exactly what we saw during the recent bear market. The S&P 500 plunged 37% in 2008, while emerging markets stocks did even worse — falling 53.3%.

From a diversification standpoint, an investor who held both U.S. and international stocks would have done better — less bad, really — than an investor who was heavily concentrated in emerging markets stocks and had little or no domestic exposure. Both investors obviously would have suffered big losses, but the diversified investor would have a smaller hole to climb out of.

Effective Diversification

To enjoy the potential benefits that diversification offers, you need to diversify effectively and intelligently. Simply buying a bunch of stocks, bonds, mutual funds or other investments doesn't automatically mean that you have dampened your portfolio's risk and enhanced its potential return. Effective diversification requires you to be thoughtful in your approach to building and maintaining your portfolio.

Too often, investors tend to simply collect investments. They buy a stock because they heard it was hot or because their uncle works for the firm, or they invest in several funds that they read about in various magazines without regard for whether those funds complement each other.

For example, say you own an index mutual fund that attempts to track the performance of the S&P 500 Index and you decide to add to your portfolio a mutual fund that tracks the Dow Jones Industrial Average. That move doesn't add any meaningful diversification benefits because both of those investments hold shares of U.S. large-company stocks. Therefore, those two investments should react similarly to new developments in the markets and the economy. When U.S. large-company stocks are down, both investments should decline — and probably by roughly the same amount, since their holdings are similar. As a result, there's nothing in your portfolio to help diminish the impact of the losses in these investments when they occur.

To avoid that type of scenario, investors need to stop simply collecting investments for random reasons and instead own assets that are designed to work together to create portfolios that are stronger than their individual components. That means holding asset classes and investments that have dissimilar price movements from each other and don't react the same way to new developments — in other words, asset classes that can "zig" when others "zag." Here's how:

1. **Diversify among large and small stocks.** We've seen that small stocks have tended to outperform large stocks over time. But that journey has not been a consistently smooth one. As shown in Exhibit 7.5 on the following page, large stocks and small stocks tend to take turns leading the performance race. What's more, small stocks can lag large stocks for years (and vice versa). For example, large stocks gained 16.5% annually from 1984-1991, while small stocks gained just 9.5% a year on average

during that time. Even if you are a firm believer in the advantages of small stocks, could you stick with an entirely small stock portfolio as you watched it lag for eight years? For the vast majority of investors, the answer is a resounding "no." Likewise, large stocks can experience years of poor performance — as they did from 1975-1982, returning 14.9% annually while small stocks soared 31.7%. Therefore, it may make sense to include both large and small stocks in the stock portion of your portfolio. Given the long-term historical outperformance of small stocks, we do believe in overweighting small versus large.

Exhibit 7.5: Small Stocks vs. Large Stocks 1972–2012

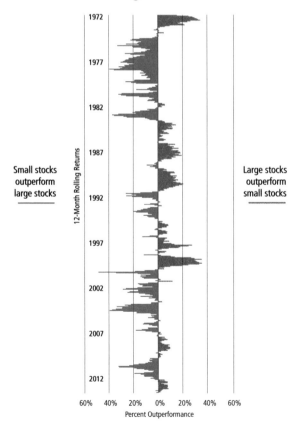

Source: DFA Returns. Large-cap stocks are represented by the Standard & Poor's 500 Index, an unmanaged market value-weighted index of 500 large company stocks that are traded on the

NYSE, AMEX and NASDAQ. S&P 500® is a registered trademark of Standard & Poor's Financial Services LLC. The Center for Research in Security Prices (CRSP) ranks all NYSE companies by market capitalization and divides them into 10 equally-populated portfolios. AMEX and NASDAQ National Market stocks are then placed into deciles according to their respective capitalizations, determined by the NYSE breakpoints. CRSP Portfolios 6-10 represent small caps. Small company stocks may be subject to a higher degree of market risk than the securities of more established companies because they may be more volatile and less liquid. Indexes are unmanaged baskets of securities without the fees and expenses associated with mutual funds and other investments. Investors cannot directly invest in an index. Past performance is not indicative of future results.

2. **Diversify among value and growth stocks.** We saw in the last chapter that value stocks have historically outperformed growth stocks over time. But just like small and large stocks, value and growth stocks each go in and out of favor — and each has a habit of going on extended runs at the expense of the other (see Exhibit 7.6 on the following page). While growth stocks as a group handily beat value stocks in aggregate from 1995-1999 (31.2% versus 21.9%, respectively), value won from 1972-1989 — gaining 16.6% versus 9.8% for growth. Again, given the long-term historical outperformance of value stocks, we do believe in overweighting value versus growth.

Exhibit 7.6: Growth Stocks vs. Value Stocks 1972 – 2012

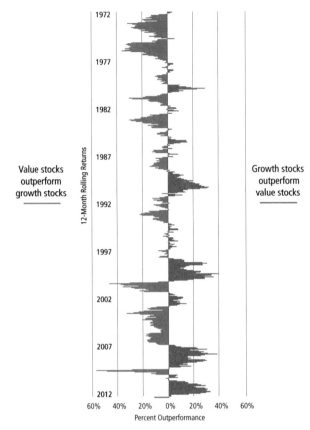

Source: DFA Returns. The Center for Research in Security Prices (CRSP) ranks all NYSE companies by market capitalization and divides them into 10 equally-populated portfolios. AMEX and NASDAQ National Market stocks are then placed into deciles according to their respective capitalizations, determined by the NYSE breakpoints. Value is represented by companies with a book-to-market ratio in the top 30% of all companies. Growth is represented by companies with a book-to-market ratio in the bottom 30% of all companies. The risks associated with investing in value stocks potentially include increased volatility (up and down movement in the value of your assets) and loss of principal. Past performance is not indicative of future results.

3. **Bring international stocks into the mix.** Events that affect U.S. companies don't always have the same impact on firms internationally. As a result, shares of overseas companies may rise when the overall U.S. market is slumping (see Exhibit 7.7). For example, international stocks returned 13.5% in 2005 — a year when the U.S. market gained just 4.9%.

Exhibit 7.7: International Stocks vs. U.S. Stocks 1972 – 2012

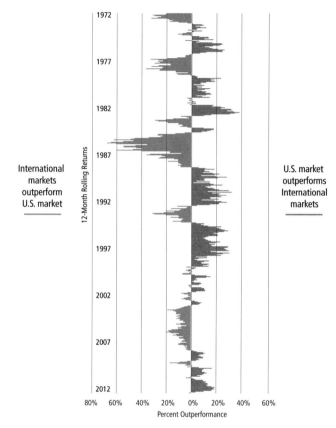

Data Source: DFA Returns. U.S. Market represented by CRSP 1-10 Index. International Markets represented by MSCI EAFE (net div.). All investments involve risk, including loss of principal. Foreign and small company securities involve additional risks. Indexes are unmanaged baskets of securities without the fees and expenses associated with mutual funds and other investments. Investors cannot directly invest in an index. Past performance is not indicative of future results.

There's another reason to diversify internationally: approximately 50% of the global stock market's value now comes from non-U.S. companies. Therefore, investors who forsake foreign investments don't own many of the world's most well known and successful companies including Royal Dutch Shell, Volkswagon, Samsung and Toyota. By adding international stocks investors can better diversify and also give themselves more opportunities to profit from the growth of capitalism across the globe.

4. Add short-term, high-quality bonds to reduce risk. Bonds are a crucial asset class for many investors, as only the more aggressive among us are comfortable owning portfolios made up entirely of stocks. Bond prices are much less volatile than stock prices and they often move in the opposite direction of stocks, making bonds an excellent potential source of diversification and risk reduction that can help protect wealth when stocks suffer. Most recently, we saw this during the market meltdown of 2008. As stocks plummeted by 37% or more, intermediate-term U.S. government bonds rose by 13%.

We believe the most effective way to diversify a stock portfolio with bonds is to buy short-term, high quality bonds to diminish the risk in the stock portfolio to an acceptable level for the overall portfolio. Bonds with longer maturities and of lower quality entail more risk than do short-term bonds of very high quality. Bonds that mature farther in the future are hit harder by unexpected increases in interest rates and inflation, while bonds with lower credit quality have a higher risk of default.

The incremental returns provided for the additional risks associated with longer maturity or lower quality have not historically compensated investors adequately for the added risk. We believe short-term, high quality bonds can be used as the brake, not the throttle, in the portfolio to control portfolio risk to the appropriate level.

Note in Exhibit 7.8 that the risk (as measured by standard deviation) of long-term bonds is much greater than the risk in Treasury bills with maturities of just one year or less. Now notice how similar the historical returns in each category are. Clearly, owning relatively volatile, long-term bonds doesn't offer much in the way of extra returns over extremely low-risk, short-term issues.

Exhibit 7.8: The Risk/Return Trade-Off in Long-Term vs. Short-Term Bonds Quarterly: 1964 – 2012

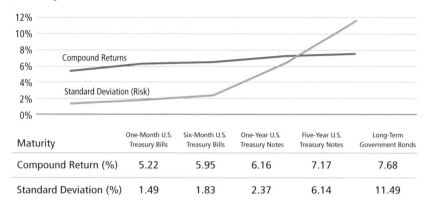

Maturity	One-Month U.S. Treasury Bills	Six-Month U.S. Treasury Bills	One-Year U.S. Treasury Notes	Five-Year U.S. Treasury Notes	Long-Term Government Bonds
Compound Return (%)	5.22	5.95	6.16	7.17	7.68
Standard Deviation (%)	1.49	1.83	2.37	6.14	11.49

Source: DFA Returns. One-Month U.S. Treasury Bills, Five-Year U.S. Treasury Notes, and Twenty-Year (Long-Term) U.S. Government Bonds provided by Ibbotson Associates. Six-Month U.S. Treasury Bills provided by CRSP (1964-1977) and B of A Merrill Lynch (1978-present). One-Year U.S. Treasury Notes provided by CRSP (1964-May 1991) and B of A Merrill Lynch (June 1991-present). Ibbotson data ©Stocks, Bonds, Bills, and Inflation Yearbook™, Ibbotson Associates, Chicago (annually updated work by Roger G. Ibbotson and Rex A. Sinquefield). CRSP data provided by the Center for Research in Security Prices, University of Chicago. The Merrill Lynch Indices are used with permission; copyright 2012 B of A Merrill Lynch, Pierce, Fenner & Smith Incorporated; all rights reserved. Assumes reinvestment of dividends. Past performance is not indicative of future results. Standard deviation annualized from quarterly data. Standard deviation is a statistical measurement of how far the return of a security (or index) moves above or below its average value. The greater the standard deviation, the riskier an investment is considered to be.

As seen in Exhibit 7.9 on the following page, bonds with lower credit ratings (such as BBB and high-yield bonds) do not tend to offer ample enough return potential over higher quality bonds to justify their additional risk.

Exhibit 7.9: The Risk/Return Trade-Off in High Quality vs. Lower Quality Bonds — Quarterly: 1983 – 2012

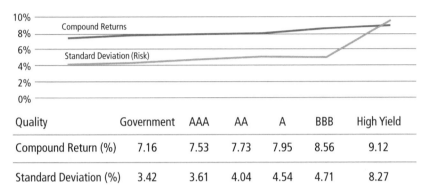

Quality	Government	AAA	AA	A	BBB	High Yield
Compound Return (%)	7.16	7.53	7.73	7.95	8.56	9.12
Standard Deviation (%)	3.42	3.61	4.04	4.54	4.71	8.27

Source: Morningstar Direct. Government rating is BarCapUS Government Intermediate Index, AAA rating is BarCap US Intermediate Credit Aaa Index. AA rating is BarCapUS Intermediate Credit Aa Index. A rating is BarCap US Intermediate Credit A Index. BBB rating is BarCap US Intermediate Credit BBB Index. High Yield rating is BarCap US High Yield Intermediate Index. Indices are not available for direct investment. Assumes reinvestment of dividends. Past performance is not indicative of future results. Standard deviation annualized from quarterly data. Standard deviation is a statistical measurement of how far the return of a security (or index) moves above or below its average value. The greater the standard deviation, the riskier an investment is considered to be.

There are two key lessons here. One is that short-term, high-quality bonds should do a much better job at decreasing the volatility of an overall portfolio than other types of bonds because their prices are more stable. That stability can help to reduce a portfolio's amount of price fluctuation. The other is that you may want to think twice before seeking to generate lots of additional return by owning long-term, low-quality bonds that require you to take on significant risk for little reward.

We hope by now that it's become clear that diversifying your portfolio is not just a smart move but can even be a liberating experience. Diversifying means that you no longer have to go through the futile and oftentimes fruitless effort of trying to predict the future and buy and sell the "right" investments. Instead you can spend your time on your business, your family or yourself.

CHAPTER 8

Building and Implementing Your Investment Portfolio

The next step in the *360 Wealth Management* process is to create a portfolio based on your particular situation and then implement it using specific investment vehicles. As you'll see in this chapter, it's also important to place those investment vehicles in the appropriate types of accounts, as well as formally document your portfolio choices and the reasons behind them by implementing an Investment Policy Statement.

Key Questions to Consider When Building Your Portfolio

To begin, you need to consider a series of issues that will help you establish the right portfolio for you — one designed to take into account your specific goals, time horizon, income needs and your comfort with investment risk.

Broadly, the issues to consider are divided into three main areas: risk capacity, risk tolerance and investment preferences.

Risk Capacity Considerations

Your capacity to bear investment risk on a purely objective basis will be determined by factors such as:

- **Your portfolio goals.** Nearly all investors have one of five primary goals: retirement funding, education funding, wealth accumulation, capital preservation or estate maximization. Of course, you may have more than one of these goals — for example, funding a comfortable retirement for yourself and your spouse while also passing on a significant portion of your assets to children and grandchildren. Therefore, you might choose to create multiple portfolios, each one designed to achieve a specific objective.

- **Your time horizon.** You must determine the approximate length of time that your money will need to be invested in order to determine an appropriate allocation to stocks in your portfolio. Because stocks can generate substantial losses over the short term, it is usually inappropriate to invest in stocks for any goal with a time horizon of five years or fewer. Generally, however, portfolios with longer-term goals have a higher capacity for stock market risk. The reason: Stock returns fluctuate less the longer you hold stocks. Indeed, as seen in Exhibit 8.1, stocks have generated positive returns during 100% of rolling 15-year periods since 1972.

Exhibit 8.1: The Range of Stock Market Returns Over Various Time Periods — S&P 500 Index Rolling Returns 1972 – 2012

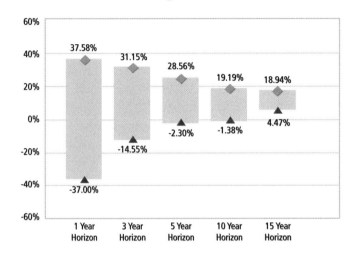

The chart above shows the maximum and minimum returns for the S&P 500 index over 12-month rolling periods since 1972. S&P 500® is a registered trademark of Standard & Poor's Financial Services LLC. Source: DFA Returns. Past performance is no guarantee of future results, and values fluctuate. Principal value, share prices and investment returns fluctuate with changes in market conditions, so that an investor's shares when redeemed or sold, may be worth more or less than their original cost. Indexes are unmanaged baskets of securities without the fees and expenses associated with mutual funds and other investments.

- **Your income requirements.** Another key factor in determining the right asset allocation is to clearly define your current income requirement from your portfolio. In addition, consider whether you will require a significant withdrawal of principal from the portfolio within the next five years to fund a major expense — such as buying a home or paying for college tuition. As a rule of thumb, you should have enough money invested in relatively stable short-term, high-quality bonds to meet three to five years' worth of major expenses and income needs.

Risk Tolerance Considerations

To create the right portfolio for your situation, you also need to consider questions that go beyond your objective ability to incur investment risk and help you assess your emotional comfort with risk. The reason: If you are not comfortable with the amount of risk in your portfolio, you may be tempted to deviate from your investment plan during periods of extreme market behavior — for example, selling out of stocks during deep bear markets and missing the benefits of future stock market rallies. The capacity to take on risk based on your goals and time horizon won't do you much good if you panic when the markets tumble and make rash changes to your portfolio that could throw off your entire financial plan.

To help you better determine your comfort level with risk, consider the following:

- **Your general approach to risk.** Do you try to avoid risk as much as possible in your life, including in non-financial areas? Would you describe yourself more as cautious or willing to take some calculated risks? Or are you generally a risk taker?

- **Your feelings about market fluctuations.** Think about watching the ups and downs in your portfolio — especially back in 2008 and early 2009 when the market was rising and falling by hundreds of points on a given day. When you think about those wild swings, do you say to yourself, "I can accept lots of ups and downs so I can maximize returns?" Or are you more likely to be willing to tolerate *some* fluctuations in the value of your portfolio in order to keep pace with inflation? Or would you rather not experience *any* fluctuations even if that means accepting lower returns that don't keep up with inflation?

- **Your reaction to market declines on your portfolio's value.** Let's say you have a portfolio worth $1 million, and a bear market causes the value of that portfolio to plummet by $300,000 over the course of a 12-month period. If you looked at your account statement and saw that your portfolio was now worth just $700,000, what would you do? Can you confidently say that you would not sell? Would you be uncertain about what to do next? Would you almost certainly sell after experiencing such a large loss in just one year? Or would you never even have invested in a portfolio that could lose so much money so quickly in the first place?

Investment Preferences

Finally, given what you've learned about the diversification benefits and the return and risk characteristics of international investments, value stocks and small stocks, how comfortable are you with owning each of these three types of investments in your portfolio? Each of these asset classes have a place in the portfolio, but if you will be uncomfortable when either or all of these asset classes are underperforming the broad U.S. market, you may want to consider adjustments to your diversification strategy to increase your overall comfort with the portfolio.

The key to success in any investment plan is the ability to stay invested for the long-term. A portfolio that's right for you should be designed to maximize potential returns for your comfort level with risk.

Implementing Your Portfolio Strategy

Investors today have more options than ever in terms of investment vehicles and products. Despite the increasing number of choices that exist, we believe that mutual funds are an excellent solution for the vast majority of investors looking to achieve their long-term goals. The major benefits of mutual funds include:

- **Diversification.** Mutual funds typically hold huge numbers of stocks and bonds — upwards of 500 in some cases — from numerous industries, and may even invest in multiple countries from around the globe. In other words, funds can provide instant diversification at a much lower cost than if you tried to create your own diversified portfolio of thousands of stocks, bonds and other investments.

- **Regulations.** Mutual funds are one of the most highly regulated investment vehicles. It is noteworthy that many of the failed Ponzi schemes and frauds that were uncovered during the Great Recession (Madoff, Stanford, Phillip Barry) were in investment products other than mutual funds.

- The mutual fund itself is registered with the SEC as an investment company under the Investment Company Act of 1940.

- A mutual fund can only be advised by an investment advisor registered with the SEC pursuant to the Investment Advisors Act of 1940.

- The shares of a mutual fund are generally securities themselves registered with the SEC pursuant to the Securities Act of 1933 and regulated per the Securities and Exchange Act of 1934.

Also, mutual funds have ticker symbols through which valuations can be determined quickly online at a financial website. More complex securities — like mortgage-backed securities, derivatives, and private placements — are not always easy to evaluate and price and therefore can be sources of abuse.

Active Versus Passive

While we have already looked at the general differences between active and passive investing, we'd like to review some additional benefits of using passive funds.

Passive funds offer the key benefit of style consistency. If you create an overall structure for your portfolio — an asset allocation strategy — you need the investments you use to stay committed to their respective investment styles. You don't want a fund that is in stocks one day, cash the next. This makes maintaining a suitable asset allocation very difficult. For that reason, active funds aren't always appropriate for investors who wish to build and maintain well thought out, diversified asset allocation strategies that require consistency.

Passive funds typically have much lower costs and management fees than active funds. That's because passive funds simply own all the stocks that make up their target index or asset class. They don't have to spend lots of time, money and human resources trying to identify the winners and losers and making numerous trades that generate costs — costs that get passed on to their shareholders.

Among passive funds, there are three main options to consider:

- **Index funds.** As you're probably aware, index funds attempt to replicate the performance of specific commercial indices (the S&P 500, the Russell 2000, the MSCI EAFE, etc.). They offer investors an easy way to gain exposure to a broad range of investment categories and styles. The downside to index funds: Since the funds need to track their indices as closely as possible, their managers must buy and sell certain stocks whenever their target index deletes or adds securities. Such trading can generate unwanted costs.

- **Exchange traded funds.** An ETF is similar to an index fund in that it seeks to mirror the holdings of a commercial index and match its performance. Because of how they're structured, however, ETFs have expenses that are often even lower than those of traditional index mutual funds. They also offer a high degree of tax efficiency. An enormous number of ETFs exist, allowing investors to build broadly diversified passive portfolios with exposure to a wide variety of investments.

- **Asset class funds.** Less well known among investors than index funds or ETFs, asset class funds attempt to deliver the investment returns of an entire broad asset class. In that respect they are extremely similar to index funds and ETFs. But unlike those two options, asset class funds don't necessarily own the exact same securities that are found in a commercial index like the S&P 500. Instead, they hold large numbers of securities with similar risk and expected return characteristics. A small-cap stock asset class fund, for example, might define small-caps somewhat differently than would an index fund or ETF that tracks the Russell 2000 index of small-company stocks. Asset class fund investors believe that these funds offer truer and more accurate exposure to various segments of the financial market.

A Word About Asset Location

Once you've created your ideal portfolio strategy and implemented your plan using specific investment vehicles, you still have another important duty: deciding how to best locate your assets in your portfolio.

Asset location is all about placing each of your various investments into one of two types of accounts — taxable or non-taxable/tax-deferred — to achieve optimal tax efficiency, defer taxes and generate the best after-tax returns possible. The best location for your assets depends on factors such as the tax laws at the time, the tax and return characteristics of the investments you own and your income tax bracket.

There are some general guidelines that you can use to start thinking about which of your investments are best-suited to each type of account. For example, low-cost index funds, ETFs, tax-free municipal bonds and asset class funds that don't make a lot of trades and are already highly tax efficient and thus are often placed in taxable accounts, because placing them in tax-advantaged accounts doesn't do much to minimize taxes. But investments that generate significant taxable income — such as some taxable bond funds and REIT funds — are often placed in tax-deferred or non-taxable accounts to help minimize current tax liabilities. There is no one "right" answer when it comes to asset location. Your specific needs, circumstances and tax situation should drive the decision.

Put It in Writing

The final step in establishing your portfolio is to create an Investment Policy Statement. This is a written document spelling out the key components of your financial situation and investment plan, and the reasons behind why you have structured your portfolio the way you have. It should contain your answers to the types of questions outlined earlier in this chapter — answers regarding your goals, time horizon, risk tolerance and ability to withstand risk, liquidity and income requirements, and your approach to your portfolio's asset allocation and investment vehicles.

By putting this information in writing, you'll clarify what goals you are hoping to achieve by investing and why you have chosen to use the approach you are using. Such clarity can be extremely beneficial to you — both when markets are soaring and possibly tempting you to chase hot market sectors and also when markets are plummeting and perhaps tempting you to cash out of stocks and deviate from your plan. An Investment Policy Statement can help you avoid the worst and most dangerous emotional reactions to various market developments. For that reason, we strongly encourage you to have an Investment Policy Statement that you can refer to whenever you think it's time to make big changes to your portfolio or overall saving and investing strategy. It may be one of the most valuable documents you'll ever use.

CHAPTER 9

Invest for the Long Term

By creating and implementing a portfolio strategy around your needs and preferences, you've put yourself on a sound path toward achieving your investment goals. However, your job isn't finished. In fact, you now must contend with perhaps the biggest challenge you'll ever face as an investor: avoiding the foolish mistakes that can jeopardize your financial future.

As investors — and as human beings, really — we are predisposed to constantly take action. We're always racing around trying to "get ahead of the curve." It's counterintuitive in our culture to believe that doing nothing is in any way a better idea than doing something.

And yet, when it comes to investing, being overactive is the downfall of too many investors. That's why one of the smartest moves you can make is to be patient and disciplined regarding your portfolio and your wealth management plan. This means doing less, not more. It means exercising restraint instead of charging ahead. And it means staying focused on what is truly important to your life goals and ignoring the enormous amount of emotion and "noise" that too often clouds investors' judgment and prompts them to make rash moves that hurt their chances of achieving all that is important to them.

As you'll see in this chapter, a long-term perspective is a key driver of investment success. But it's also a task that can be extraordinarily difficult to achieve because of our hard-wired tendencies. The good news: There are steps you can take that will help you be a more patient and disciplined investor.

The Importance of Staying Invested

Once you've built your portfolio and are invested the way you want to be, it's critical to stick with your plan and not jump in and out of various investments and asset classes. The reason: Deviating from your disciplined approach by being out of a particular market segment can decimate your portfolio's long-term returns.

Consider Exhibit 9.1, which shows the performance of the S&P 500 from 1970-2012. The index during that entire four decade period generated an annualized compound return of 9.94%. If you owned an index or asset class fund that tracked the S&P 500 and matched its returns over that entire period, you would have earned the same return (minus expenses).

If, however, you traded actively and moved in and out of the fund, your returns would most likely have suffered. By missing just the single best day for the S&P 500 during those 43 years — that's one day out of 43 years — your annualized return would have fallen to 9.66%. And if you had missed the best 15 days over that entire period, you would have earned a mere 7.47% on your investment. Put in dollar terms, the difference is even more startling. If you'd stayed in the market for the whole period, your $100,000 would have grown to $5,884,323. Missing the best 15 days in that period would have cut your returns almost in two-thirds to $2,214,888. Missing just five of the best days would have cut your returns by $2 million to $3,818,624, a stark illustration of the dangers of trying to time the markets.

Exhibit 9.1: The Effect of Missing the Market's Best Days
"Time In" vs. "Timing" the Market — Performance of the S&P 500
Index 1970 – 2012

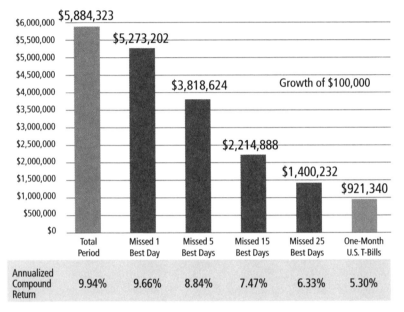

Annualized Compound Return	9.94%	9.66%	8.84%	7.47%	6.33%	5.30%

Source: The S&P data are provided by Standard & Poor's Index Services Group. US bonds and bills data ©2012 Stocks, Bonds, Bills, and Inflation Yearbook™, Ibbotson Associates, Chicago (annually updated work by Roger G. Ibbotson and Rex A. Sinquefield). Indexes are not available for direct investment. Their performance does not reflect the expenses associated with the management of an actual portfolio. S&P 500® is a registered trademark of Standard & Poor's Financial Services LLC.

The upshot: A relatively small number of trading days tends to be responsible for the stock market's strong returns over time. Miss even a handful of those days and you stand to end up with a lot less wealth than you would if you simply stayed "all-in" the entire time.

Of course, it's tempting to think about the flip-side of this situation and wonder what would happen if you avoided the market's very worst days over time. In that case, your returns would look a lot different. However, you've got to ask yourself: Do I feel lucky? Are you agile enough to avoid the market's very worst days year in and year out over several decades? And after you've avoided those down days, are you also astute enough to get back in to the market in time to catch the next big "up" day? To test yourself, answer the following two questions:

- How was my portfolio allocated on October 15, 2008? On that day, the S&P 500 plummeted 9% — one of its worst single-day performances in the past 40 years. Did you see that day coming and shift your portfolio out of U.S. stocks to avoid the damage? Or did it hit you unexpectedly?

- How was my portfolio allocated on October 28, 2008? On that date — just 13 days after one of the S&P 500's worst single-day performances — the index delivered one of its best single-day performances, soaring 10.8%. Think back. Did you know that was about to happen and therefore get back into stocks or increase your allocation to stocks? Or were you, like most other investors, still worried about the possibility of a global financial meltdown?

If you got it wrong, don't feel badly: You had plenty of company. Investors time and time again get nervous or impatient and break their discipline — typically at exactly the wrong times.

As a result of such ill-timed shifting of money, investors experience substantially lower returns than what the market offers them. For example, while the S&P 500 gained 8.21% annually from 1993-2012, the average stock fund investor gained just 4.25% a year on average — that's a full 4 percentage points less than the index (see Exhibit 9.2).

Exhibit 9.2: Market Rates of Return vs. Investors' Actual Rates of Return Average Investor vs. Major Indices 1993 – 2012

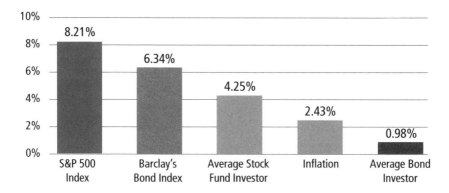

Average stock investor and average bond investor performances were used from a DALBAR study, Quantitative Analysis of Investor Behavior (QAIB), 03/2013. QAIB calculates investor returns as the change in assets after excluding sales, redemptions, and exchanges. This method of calculation captures realized and unrealized capital gains, dividends, interest, trading costs, sales charges, fees, expenses, and any other costs. After calculating investor returns in dollar terms (above), two percentages are calculated: Total investor return rate for the period and annualized investor return rate. Total return rate is determined by calculating the investor return dollars as a percentage of the net of the sales, redemptions, and exchanges for the period. The fact that buy-and-hold has been a successful strategy in the past does not guarantee that it will continue to be successful in the future.

The damage of missing 4 percentage points of return a year on average is devastating. $100,000 invested in an S&P index fund that earned 8.21% annually would grow to $484,560 in 20 years (not accounting for fees, taxes or expenses). However, if you'd invested like the average stock investor in this study, and earned a 4.25% annual return, you'd only have $229,891. The $254,669 difference between these two results is a dramatic demonstration of the potential value of patience and discipline. Bond investors fared even worse. While the Barclay's bond index gained 6.34% annually from 1993-2012, the average bond fund investor realized an annualized gain of just 0.98% — less than the average rate of inflation during that period.

The upshot: Investors are trading too frequently. They are chasing after hot investments just as those investments are about to go cold. And they are avoiding investments that are positioned to post strong gains. If they weren't, they would perform at least as well as the indices, if not better — and clearly they're not.

The Challenge of Staying Disciplined

There's a good reason why investors tend to consistently make these and other mistakes with their money. As human beings, we have ingrained tendencies to let our short-term emotions guide our longer-term decisions, such as investing.

For example, strong emotions can quickly cause us to misinterpret facts and make the wrong moves at the wrong time — repeatedly.

To see how this cycle of emotions plays out in real life, consider Exhibit 9.3. It shows a hypothetical example of what happens to many investors. When the market is on the rise and racking up big gains, investors quickly change from being optimistic to excited to downright elated. They eventually start to worry that they're being left behind by not buying stocks — that their friends are all getting rich and that they better invest heavily in stocks in order to look smart and make money. So after spending weeks or even months watching the stock market post strong returns, they buy in or ramp up their allocation to stocks.

Typically what happens is that shortly thereafter the market starts to show signs of weakness and begins to fall. At first, investors might be a bit concerned about these developments, but they find reassurance by telling themselves that "it's only a temporary setback." But it isn't. Stock prices continue to decline and investors become alarmed and frightened — with a growing certainty that "it's different this time" and that stocks have become a sucker's bet that will never pay off. As that fear really kicks in, they sell their stocks and buy bonds.

If you paid attention at all during the past few years, you know what typically happens next. Stocks begin to rally once again — often unexpectedly posting outsized gains in a very short window of time.

Exhibit 9.3: The Cycle of Market Emotions

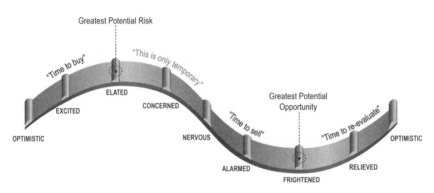

For illustration purposes only

The bottom line for too many investors is that they buy at the top, driven by elation and greed. They then sell out at the bottom and lock in their losses, driven by fear. And they miss the start of the next upswing.

This cycle will no doubt look familiar to many of you. But the question remains: Why do we let our emotions replace our capacity for rational thought and drive our investment decisions in the first place?

The answer lies in a field of academic and economic study called behavioral finance, which studies the many biological and psychological factors that drive our decision-making processes. We like to think of ourselves as fairly rational, but behavioral finance shows otherwise.

Behavioral finance is a fascinating and rapidly evolving field of study. Information about how investors really make decisions is being researched all the time. However, work in this important new field — some of which has won the Nobel Prize in economics — has identified several key ways in which our brains trick us into seeing the investment world one way, when in reality it's something quite different. These cognitive biases include:

- **Anchoring bias.** This reflects our tendency to latch our thinking onto a reference point that we are familiar with — even if that reference point isn't relevant to our particular situation. In an investment context, we tend to "anchor" to the long-term average return of stocks and expect stock returns in any given year to approximate the average. But, of course, stock returns in any given year may be wildly different from the long-term average. This conflicts with our mental "anchor," which causes us to panic and make bad investment decisions when returns are negative in a single year or get extremely exuberant when returns are abnormally high.

- **Confirmation bias.** Too often we look only for evidence that confirms our existing beliefs while ignoring or discounting evidence that shows them to be false or questionable. If you think a potential investment is going to be a huge winner, you'll probably seek out other opinions that match yours and believe that people with conflicting beliefs "just don't get it." The investment could be a dog in many ways, but you're not willing to hear it. The result, too often, is a sizeable investment loss. A good historical example of this was in the high-technology stock boom of the late 1990s. Many investors over-allocated their investment capital to high tech stocks, ignoring both their risk profiles and the key principles of diversification. The resulting decline in these technology stocks had a greater effect on investors who had concentrated much of their wealth to this industry.

- **Hindsight bias.** Often we feel that whatever happened was bound to happen — that luck or chance couldn't play a part in a given situation and that ultimately, everything that occurred could have been predicted. If stock prices fall after a long bull run, it must have been because "trees don't grow to the sky" — we knew it all along. But if stock prices continue to rise, it's because "the trend is your friend." Looking back on investments' past performance, it's natural for us to think that we — or someone — should have seen it coming and taken the appropriate action.

For example, think back to the technology stock bubble. With the elapsed time, it's easy for an investor to acknowledge there was a bubble and that stock prices had to plummet. But at the time, most investors either a) didn't see a bubble, b) saw it but didn't do anything to protect themselves or c) felt that "it's different this time." Hindsight bias often leads to a sense of overconfidence, making investors think they're much smarter or adept at picking stocks than they really are. Another name for hindsight bias is "Monday morning quarterbacking," named for the tendency for football fans to see so clearly what decisions coaches should have made in the games on Sunday.

By understanding these and other cognitive biases that affect us all, you can do a better a job of recognizing your particular biases and try hard to overcome any urges to act on your short-term emotions. It's not always easy to notice your biases and shut them down, of course. But if you can keep your emotions in check when making investment decisions, you'll find yourself in much better shape down the road.

The Need to Review and Rebalance

Keep in mind that patience and discipline don't mean burying your head in the sand and doing nothing at all. The point is to do only those things that will maximize your chances of having a successful investment experience, and no more.

Take rebalancing. When you review your portfolio's performance, rebalancing should be a key strategy on your list. As financial markets and asset classes rise and fall, your portfolio's exposure to stocks, bonds, cash and other investments will fluctuate as well. Over time, your overall target asset allocations will shift — leaving you with more money invested in stocks than you prefer, for example, and less invested in bonds. The result: You may find that your portfolio now carries more investment risk than you feel comfortable with or need.

Rebalancing is one of the keys to keeping your portfolio on track and maintaining the right balance between growth potential and risk exposure. Rebalancing your portfolio back to its target allocation helps to control the level of risk in your portfolio, and has historically shown to provide more growth of wealth over time because it is essentially a process of buying low and selling high. A disciplined rebalancing schedule will also help to remove emotions from investment decision making.

Rebalancing is a relatively straightforward, easy process to implement. Let's say you have $500,000 invested. Based on your goals and risk profile, you want your portfolio to have a long-term target asset allocation of 60% stocks and 40% bonds. Initially, $300,000 would be allocated to stocks and $200,000 would be allocated to bonds. If your stock holdings gained 10% over the next 12 months and your bond holdings lost 5%, your asset allocation would then be 63% stocks (worth $330,000) and 37% bonds (worth $190,000). To get back to your target 60/40 mix, you would need to sell a portion of your stocks and reallocate the proceeds to your bond holdings.

Two recent periods in market history show the potential advantages of rebalancing back to a target asset mix. In the late 1990s, large-company growth stocks and technology stocks were posting huge gains. An investor using a disciplined approach to rebalancing would have sold some of those stocks as they soared in value and reinvested the proceeds into bonds in order to keep their desired allocation between stocks and bonds. This would have benefited the investor in two ways: When tech and large-cap stocks began plummeting in 2000, the investor would have avoided some of the worst losses. Additionally, by maintaining his target bond allocation, he would have been well positioned to benefit from the strong gains that bonds began generating as stocks fell.

Also consider the more recent bear market that occurred in 2008 and its effect on a hypothetical static portfolio that is never rebalanced. For example, a portfolio of 50% stocks (S&P 500) and 50% bonds (five-year Treasury notes) in 1987 would have shifted to an allocation of 73% stocks and 27% bonds by the end of 2007 — making the portfolio significantly riskier than the original 50/50 portfolio. The return on this more aggressive portfolio would have been a whopping -23.6% in 2008. By contrast, the return on the 50/50 portfolio would have been -12% — a difference of 11.6 percentage points.

Of course, 2008 wasn't a comfortable time for any investor. But if you had to choose between a regularly rebalanced portfolio with a negative 12% return or a portfolio that was never rebalanced and lost nearly 24%, chances are you'd be a lot more comfortable with the first option. And as we've seen, your comfort level with and commitment to your investment plan is vitally important. If you can emotionally withstand the ups and downs in your portfolio, you're far less likely to take reckless actions like jumping in and out of the market, or falling victim to some of the cognitive biases highlighted previously.

But comfort is only one reason why it makes sense to reduce risk through rebalancing. Lower volatility also means that your portfolio can regain any ground it's lost during bad market environments faster than it could otherwise. For example, say your portfolio declines by 20% during a bear market. To get back to where you started, you'd actually need to earn a 25% return. And if it fell by 50%, you would need a return of 100% just to get back to where you stood before that decline.

Your rebalancing decisions can be made as part of your overall portfolio review, which should be done regularly depending on your preferences and the complexity of your portfolio. If, during your review, you see that your portfolio's current allocation to any single asset class is significantly higher than your target allocation to that asset class (say, 3-5% or more), you might sell some of those assets to realign with your target. Likewise, if you see that your exposure to an asset class is 3-5% lower than your target, you might buy more of that investment. By creating strict rebalancing parameters like these, you can more easily overcome the tendency to make rebalancing decisions based on emotions about the current market environment.

Your overall portfolio review should also go beyond rebalancing and determine if there have been any major developments in your life or financial situation that necessitate making changes to your overall portfolio. For example, a new child or grandchild could mean it's time to change the beneficiary designations on your investment accounts, or set up a college savings plan. A new job may mean that you can now increase the amount of money you save toward your long-term goals. It's these types of major developments that should guide your portfolio strategy decisions — not the short-term fluctuations of the markets or your emotional responses to them.

Staying On Track

Being disciplined about our investments is difficult even for the most patient among us. Despite our best intentions, the emotions that rise up in us during extreme market environments can quickly override logic and cause us to make poor decisions with our money. That's why it makes sense to arm yourself with as many tools as possible in order to help you maintain your discipline and stay on track in the face of market volatility.

One such tool is an Investment Policy Statement (IPS). As we discussed in Chapter 8, your IPS will serve as a written record of your investment strategy and the guidelines you have chosen to follow as an investor. It should spell out all the reasons why you have structured your portfolio as you have, and include details about your chosen approach to rebalancing your portfolio. During every portfolio review, your IPS can remind you of the key facts and tenets of your investment plan — which can help you avoid making short-sighted, emotionally-driven decisions. In addition, an IPS should contain historical high and low returns for your type of portfolio. This data can be invaluable during a market downturn. For example, say your portfolio is down 20% over the past year — a return that could make you panic and sell a big chunk of your investments. However, a review of your IPS might remind you that historically, a portfolio like yours experienced a decline as large as 35% over a one-year period. In light of that information, a 20% decline could be seen not as an extreme or unlikely event but instead as well within the range of possibility — helping you put the situation in historical perspective and stick with your plan.

A second important resource for investors is a fee-based wealth advisor. As the name suggests, fee-based advisors charge clients a fee for their services and are therefore not compensated by commissions on sales of investments. As a result, fee-based advisors' interests are aligned with their clients' interests: The advisors do well only if clients' portfolios do well. That means a fee-based advisor is highly motivated to give you the best advice for your situation at all times — even if that advice is to sit tight and do nothing.

Indeed, one of the biggest ways advisors add value is by bringing discipline to your investing. As we've seen, it's all too easy to let both good and bad events cause us to make changes to our portfolios. Having an advisor to guide you through those ups and downs can help you stay on course and avoid the mistake of breaking your discipline. In that sense, think of an advisor in the same way you might think of a dietician or a personal trainer — as someone who helps you set up a plan, then watches and motivates you to keep doing the right thing so you end up with the results you want. In an advisor's case, you might not lose weight or gain strength — but you might just end up making more money than you would otherwise. In Chapter 13, you'll find information that can help you assess your needs and determine what type of advisor and level of service will suit you best.

CHAPTER 10

Advanced Planning

The right investment plan is important to your financial well-being, but it is far from the only thing that matters. In order to maximize your potential for success, most of us need to look beyond investments.

That means accurately identifying the key financial risks you face and then determining the best strategies for decreasing or eliminating them. In short, you need to bring Advanced Planning into the mix and make it part of your overall plan.

Advanced Planning focuses on four key areas (see Exhibit 10.1).

Exhibit 10.1: Key Advanced Planning Concerns

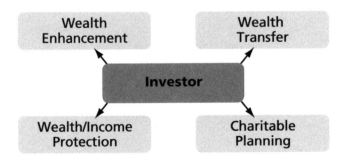

Let's look at how you might develop a plan for addressing challenges in each of these areas.

Wealth Enhancement

This is the process of maximizing the tax efficiency of your assets and cash flow as well as minimizing fees and unnecessary costs. It includes:

- **Get organized and consolidate accounts.** Before you can maximize the effectiveness of your wealth, you need to get a handle on your personal financial situation. A comprehensive list of all assets and liabilities, as well as income and expenses, should be the starting point for this process. Investors often find that they have numerous investment and bank accounts spread out across multiple fund companies, advisors, banks and brokerage firms. They also might have 401(k) or other retirement accounts from previous jobs, still with their previous employers.

  Trimming down the number of financial relationships you have can help simplify your life. Also, by consolidating all of your investment assets with a single firm and meeting a specific minimum, you may be eligible for lower overall pricing on the management of those assets. Likewise, allocating more money to one bank could allow you to earn higher interest rates.

- **Review tax returns.** The importance of having a good accountant (CPA) should not be overlooked. Your CPA should work with you (and your other advisors) to ensure that they have all relevant financial information in order to accurately project your current tax liability, and avoid underpayment penalties and interest. Additionally, your CPA may recommend strategies that can reduce your taxable income.

- **Assess cash management strategies.** You also might examine the effectiveness of your cash management strategies. Are you earning the maximum amount possible on your short-term cash (consistent with your need for safety and liquidity, of course), or could you put your cash to work more effectively? Many banks and investment firms offer "sweep" accounts that can link up your checking and money market accounts — the majority of your funds are kept in interest earning accounts, with transfers made to your checking accounts as needed.

- **Maximize use of qualified retirement plans and IRAs.** Ensure that you are contributing as much as possible to qualified plans such as 401(k)s, 403(b)s or 457 plans. Examine retirement plan options such as IRAs and Roth IRAs to determine their potential as a way to generate tax-deferred or tax-free retirement income. Also, consider converting existing IRA assets to a Roth IRA. This strategy requires tax to be paid at the time of conversion, but eliminates the need to pay taxes as funds are withdrawn. Additionally, there are no required minimum distributions for Roth IRAs, so these funds can continue to grow for the benefit of your heirs.

- **Evaluate corporate plans.** Make a point to analyze all executive compensation programs or benefit plans to ensure that they are being maximized on both a tax and benefits basis.

- **Determine ideal asset location.** As we discussed in Chapter 8, owning certain types of assets in taxable accounts and other types in nontaxable or tax-deferred accounts can reduce your tax burden significantly over time. These asset location decisions will come down to factors such as the amount of taxable income an investment tends to generate, your marginal income tax rate and capital gains tax rates.

- **Consider your own "environment."** For investors who are approaching retirement or already retired, wealth can be enhanced through cost- and tax-cutting measures such as trading down to a smaller home or relocating to a state with lower taxes.

Wealth Transfer

Proper estate planning is the most effective way to help ensure that you are able to pass along assets in ways that satisfy your wishes and provide for the financial health and well-being of your family. It also can reduce or prevent much of the stress that so often occurs when heirs attempt to sort out a family member's estate.

Many people assume that estate planning is only for the very wealthiest. This is simply not the case. Even if your net worth is relatively small, you need basic legal documents that give instructions for how you want your assets distributed at your death or if you become incapacitated. Of course, estate planning often gets ignored because it involves considering your own mortality and what will occur after you die (two topics that many of us prefer to avoid). But by asking some tough questions now — How should assets be distributed at death? How and when should heirs receive an inheritance? — you can ensure that your wishes are carried out and that your assets are distributed in the most efficient manner.

While tax and legal advice unique to your situation is beyond the scope of this book, there are some key wealth transfer action steps that you may want to consider implementing. We recommend discussing these steps with your financial advisor and other professionals to determine if they make sense for your particular situation.

- **Create/review your will.** Without a will, you face the risks that your assets won't go to whom you want. If you are married, for example, you might assume that all of your possessions will simply go to your spouse when you die. However, surviving spouses automatically inherit everything in only some states. Additionally, a will allows you to appoint a guardian for your minor children in the event of your death. Without a will, your children will be considered wards of the state, and the court will decide who will act as guardian. If you already have a will, review it every few years to ensure that it remains relevant and true to your wishes.

- **Review beneficiary designations and asset vestings.** A beneficiary designation on a bank account, life insurance policy, investment account and the like is the ultimate and overriding determinant in how the assets are transferred at death — even if your will or other documents state that the assets should go elsewhere. The upshot: Make sure that your beneficiary designations on all accounts are accurate, up-to-date and reflect your wishes. Additionally, make sure that the vesting of all assets is accurate. For example, if you have created a family trust, make sure that the assets contributed to the trust are re-titled in the trust's name.

- **Create a living will.** This is a document that spells out the specific actions you want (and don't want) taken in regard to your health care in case you can't make such decisions because of illness or incapacity. By creating clarity, such wills can save your family pain, uncertainty and money. In some states, this document is called an advance health care directive.

- **Consider various trusts.** One example is a revocable living trust, which can help your assets avoid probate. Avoiding probate saves money and also prevents the details of your estate from becoming public information. You might also consider trusts designed to pass on assets in ways that reduce estate and gift taxes — including irrevocable life insurance trusts and qualified terminable interest property trusts. These more complex trust options require the help of an estate planning attorney who can set up the trusts in accordance with all applicable laws.

- **Review life insurance opportunities.** Ownership of life insurance policies by a trust or family member other than the insured will ensure that the policy and its proceeds are not considered part of your estate. Since life insurance rates change over time and insurers create additional enhancements to policies, it is important to have existing policies reviewed every few years. Oftentimes, an existing policy can be exchanged for a new, less expensive or enhanced policy with no tax effect to the owner of the policy.

- **Consider making annual gifts.** Some smart wealth transfer strategies can be implemented while you are alive. You can make direct gifts to anyone up to a certain amount without incurring a tax bill or eroding your lifetime exemption. This has the potential to reduce the size of your taxable estate in the process.

- **Explore the possible advantage of "wealth shifting."** There are a variety of techniques that can serve as vehicles to transfer wealth from one generation to the next while minimizing both estate and gift taxes. These techniques allow assets that may have a current "low" valuation to be transferred to the next generation in hopes that the valuation increases over time; in this case, you have shifted potential future capital gains out of your estate.

- **Involve family members where possible.** Review the opportunities in any family-controlled business or investment entities for younger generation family members to "learn on the job" and be compensated as they develop valuable employment skills for the future. Additionally, ensure that the next generation is educated about the fundamentals of wealth and especially about the responsibilities and obligations that come with the transfer of sizable wealth.

Wealth and Income Protection

This involves employing strategies to ensure that your wealth is not subjected to claims from potential creditors, litigants, ex-spouses and children's spouses, as well as to protect against catastrophic losses and identity fraud.

It is best to start by evaluating all current insurance policies to determine if you are over- or under-insured for certain coverages, then decide if there are areas of coverage you are missing that need to be addressed. Some types of insurance to consider include:

- **Insurance on your home, car and other assets.** You need enough liability insurance to protect your wealth as well as adequate property insurance for your belongings. You should make sure that your insurance coverage includes all perils applicable to each asset (such as fire, flood, earthquake, hurricane, etc.).

- **Long-term disability insurance.** If a major disability prevented you from working, this insurance would help replace the job-related income you would lose. In particular, younger, high-income earners should consider disability insurance.

- **Long-term care insurance.** The costs associated with an extended nursing home stay or home health care services can decimate wealth quickly. Long-term care insurance is becoming an increasingly important area of coverage, especially as the millions of baby boomers enter their retirement years.

Business owners might also want to consider strategies to protect their wealth and the value of their businesses. Some options to consider include:

- **Buy-sell agreement.** This is a type of agreement between co-owners of a business that details what happens to the firm if a co-owner dies, becomes disabled or leaves the business. Typically funded with life and/or disability insurance, it can help to ensure business continuity and protect the wealth that has been built up in a business over time.

- **Ownership structures.** Various types of trusts and partnerships — such as family limited partnerships — can effectively place assets out of reach of creditors or make it extremely difficult for them to collect money. Likewise, structuring a business as a corporation or as a Limited Liability Company can protect owners from being named in a lawsuit against their company. Even though these ownership structures can limit personal liability, they do not eliminate the need for liability insurance coverage for the entity itself.

Other protection strategies that may be worth considering include:

• **Pre- and post-nuptial agreements.** Some couples, either before or after they are married, choose to enter into a formal, written contract that spells out how property will be divided as well as the terms of spousal support in the event of a divorce. These agreements are especially important to consider when one spouse is significantly wealthier than the other. Each party to the agreement should engage his or her own legal representative in order to avoid conflicts and issues in the future.

• **Identify theft protection strategies.** Effective low-tech actions that can protect you include: reducing the amount of crucial ID and information you carry in your wallet or purse, keeping documents like your Social Security card and passport at home and shredding account statements and financial documents. High-tech solutions include sending financial information only over a guaranteed secure connection, never responding to unsolicited "phisher" emails requesting personal information, installing and updating anti-virus, anti-spam and anti-malware software on your computer and downloading security patches to your computer that can help block intruders. There are also services available that can notify you anytime your credit report has been accessed, allowing you to prevent unauthorized use of your identity for fraudulent purposes.

Charitable Planning

This, of course, involves ways to help you fulfill any philanthropic goals you might have and maximize the effectiveness of your charitable intent. Commonly used charitable planning strategies that you should review include:

• **Outright cash gifts.** Direct gifts of cash to qualified charities are deductible for income tax purposes (up to a certain percentage of your adjusted gross income and assuming you itemize and have the proper documentation). Gifts also help to reduce the value of your estate for estate tax purposes.

- **Gifts of appreciated assets.** By donating assets, such as stocks, that have risen in value directly to a charity, you can generally avoid the capital gains tax you would incur if you sold the asset first and then donated the cash proceeds. This technique is especially valuable for individuals who have large unrealized capital gain positions in specific investments.

- **Donor-advised funds.** Donor-advised funds are pooled investments owned and controlled by a sponsoring organization. You, as the donor, make an irrevocable contribution to the fund and receive an immediate tax deduction. The fund invests the money, while allowing you to recommend specific donations, and the donor-advised fund makes the grant. The costs and administrative responsibilities of using such a fund are typically much less than running a private foundation.

- **Private foundations.** Charitably-minded investors who are relatively affluent and who want the maximum level of control over their gifting often choose to set up their own private foundation. Private foundations enable donors to control the investment of assets and strategies for grants and gifts. However, private foundations are more expensive to operate than other options and include more rules and regulations (and therefore more administrative duties) than other philanthropic vehicles. Private foundations can be appropriate for families who would like to leave a lasting legacy, enabling future generations to continue a foundation's mission for many years after the passing of the original principals.

- **Charitable trusts.** Several types of trusts allow investors to support favorite charities while generating other benefits. For example, a charitable remainder trust (CRT) enables you to gift assets to the trust. You would receive a tax deduction and avoid paying capital gains taxes on the assets donated. You would then receive income from the trust for a period of years. Once that period of time ends, the remaining amount of assets would go to your chosen charity. Additionally, the assets are removed from your estate for tax purposes.

CHAPTER 11

Relationship Management
Coordinating Wealth Management

Identifying and addressing all of these advanced planning issues is a tall order. It becomes even more challenging when you attempt to coordinate and integrate investment portfolio decisions with wealth transfer, protection and enhancement strategies.

Making consistently sound decisions about your money requires considering all aspects of each decision, and their potential impact. More importantly, it requires that all of the professionals assisting understand your situation and act in concert.

For example, executives who decide to exercise compensatory stock options may seek the advice of a tax professional in order to determine the impact these options will have on their income and related taxes. Their CPA may suggest strategies to reduce or defer the tax due on the exercise of these options.

But what other issues may be related to this decision?

Perhaps by bringing an estate planning attorney into this discussion, additional ideas may be suggested that are in line with the client's wishes to take care of heirs or support various charities.

Most people don't have a central person coordinating the advice from different professionals. Without this central person, the burden is too often left on your shoulders.

The good news is that you don't have to go it alone. A wealth advisor assumes the role of central coordinator to manage these relationships on your behalf.

One of the most important jobs of your wealth advisor is to ensure that your financial decisions are not made in a vacuum. The best way to assure that all aspects of each decision are taken into consideration is to bring in a team of experts to work in collaboration about potential solutions. Unfortunately, in our experience, this collaboration is more the exception than the rule, even with clients who have a great deal of wealth and access to the best professionals. In many cases, their advisors have never met or even spoken to each other and the result is often a wealth plan that either has some gaping holes in it or does not correspond to what the client intended.

You may have existing relationships with other professionals, such as a CPA or attorney. Your wealth advisor should be able to collaborate with them. Alternatively, if you do not currently work with these types of professionals, your advisor should be able to make recommendations to qualified specialists that he or she works with on a regular basis.

The composition of an advanced planning network usually consists of the following professionals:

- **Wealth Advisor** — Generally speaking, the wealth advisor is responsible for defining your goals, identifying your values and orchestrating the rest of your team. It is generally the wealth advisor who is in closest contact with the client and determines how best to utilize other specialists.

- **Tax Professional/CPA** — Your CPA or other tax professional will be in charge of tax planning, preparation and compliance and will work closely with your wealth advisor to ensure that decisions made regarding your investment portfolio take into consideration all relevant tax issues. In addition, your CPA will work closely with the estate planning attorney to maximize tax saving strategies in a variety of common estate planning techniques.

- **Estate Planning Attorney** — The estate planning attorney is responsible for the legal framework and documents involved in issues such as the creation of an estate plan, gifting strategies, asset protection, philanthropic consulting, and business and succession planning for entrepreneurs and business owners.

- **Insurance Specialist** — In this area, there may be multiple insurance specialists who need to be consulted. One specialist typically focuses on life, health, disability, and long-term care insurance, while another concentrates on property and casualty insurance. While it may be possible to find this expertise in one firm, it is more common for insurance professionals to specialize in one or the other. Regardless, we believe it it is important to work with an insurance broker (or brokers) rather than insurance agents. A broker works for you (the client) and can place coverage with multiple insurance companies, while an agent is a representative of a specific company.

Depending on your unique needs, there might be other professionals who you need to consult with on a semi-regular basis. For example, if you are a business owner, you may need a specialist in business valuations to value your privately-held business in the case of a proposed sale or for estate planning purposes. If you need expertise on pension and retirement plan issues, you may consult with an Actuary.

You should be able to rely on the members of your core advanced planning team to bring in some of these outside experts as needed, rather than needing to have direct relationships with professionals you may only work with once or twice.

Exhibit 11.1 on the following page shows the depth and breadth of an advanced planning team.

Exhibit 11.1: The Range of Relationships

As you can see, having your wealth advisor orchestrate your overall wealth plan can ensure that appropriate experts are being consulted as needed, and, more importantly, they are working together in close collaboration to identify all the specific risks you face as well as the full range of solutions to mitigate those risks.

Clearly, tremendous value can be realized by building a comprehensive plan that addresses both investment-related matters and non-investment concerns in a coordinated manner using appropriate experts. That, essentially, is what *360 Wealth Management* is all about — providing solutions to investors' full range of financial issues and integrating those solutions in a way that enables investors to achieve all that is truly important to them in all areas of their lives.

In the next chapter, we'll pull together everything we've shown you so far about *360 Wealth Management* so you can incorporate it into your own life and make the best possible choices about your wealth.

CHAPTER 12

Putting It All Together

Now you're ready to begin implementing the components of *360 Wealth Management*. Before you begin, however, take a moment to review the key steps in the process.

Discovery

The first step toward developing a plan that helps you accomplish what you most want is to determine those goals and values that are most important to you, and what you consider to be the biggest challenges you face.

Armed with a clear, detailed understanding of these issues, you can set out to create the ideal wealth plan for you — one that will serve as a guide to every financial decision you make.

As discussed previously, the key to developing this understanding is a Discovery Process which aligns life issues with financial issues, in order to ensure that your needs, opportunities, goals and concerns are factored into your overall wealth plan.

Create Your Investment Plan

The creation of your investment policy should be driven by the following key guidelines:

- **Markets work.** Capital markets generally work in such an efficient manner that it is extraordinarily difficult to consistently outperform the market. We believe a better approach is to simply attempt to capture the rate of return that the market offers over time — and the way to do that is extremely-broad global diversification.

- **Risk and return are related.** As an investor, it's important to take only those risks that have been shown over time to reward investors consistently.

  Bottom line: We believe that your investment strategy should center around three major decisions. First, how much money you will allocate to stocks versus to bonds, T-bills and cash. Second, how much of your stock portfolio you will allocate to value stocks versus growth stocks. And third, how much money you will allocate to small-cap stocks versus large-cap stocks.

- **Diversify with structure.** When it comes to investing, risk cannot be eliminated, but it can potentially be reduced through the philosophy of structured diversification:

  1. **Combine multiple asset classes** that have historically experienced dissimilar return patterns across a variety of market periods.

  2. **Diversify globally** — More than 60% of global stock market value is non-U.S., and international stock markets as a whole have historically experienced dissimilar return patterns to the U.S.

  3. **Invest in thousands of securities** to limit portfolio losses by reducing company-specific risk.

  4. **Invest in high-quality, short-term bonds.** Consider shorter maturities that have negative correlations historically with stocks. And lower default risk with high-quality instruments.

- **Determine the appropriate portfolio for your specific situation.** The right portfolio for you will take into account your specific goals, time horizon, income and liquidity needs, and your ability and willingness to take on investment risk in pursuit of your objectives. Structuring your portfolio on these issues will help ensure that your portfolio provides you with the appropriate balance between potential risk and return so that you can stick with your plan during a variety of market cycles in order to reach your financial goals.

Create Your Advanced Plan

A formal investment plan, while critically important, is just one component of a *360 Wealth Management* plan. A *360 Wealth Management* plan will incorporate your investment plan with other key non-investment related issues.

- **Wealth Enhancement.** This is a process of maximizing the tax efficiency of current assets and cash flow as well as minimizing fees and unnecessary costs (while achieving both growth and preservation goals).

- **Wealth Transfer.** This process can ensure that you are able to pass along assets in a tax-efficient manner and that satisfy your wishes in providing for the financial health and well-being of your family.

- **Wealth and Income Protection.** This involves employing strategies, such as trusts and insurance, to ensure that your wealth is not subjected to claims from potential creditors, litigants, ex-spouses and children's spouses, as well as protecting against catastrophic losses and identity fraud.

- **Charitable Planning.** This, of course, involves ways to help you fulfill any philanthropic goals you might have and maximize the effectiveness of your charitable intent.

Invest for the Long Term

Taking a long term approach and exercising patience and discipline are in many ways the most important determinants of your eventual financial success or failure. It's therefore vital that you stick to your plan — especially during periods when the financial markets are extremely volatile.

Of course, remaining patient and disciplined can be extremely difficult when stocks or other assets are soaring or plummeting. The way our brains are hard-wired can cause us to make emotional decisions about our money at precisely the wrong moments — such as buying hot stocks right before they're about to fall and selling stocks just before they're about to rally — that can damage our financial plan.

The solution is to build safeguards into your plan that help you stay focused on the long term and tune out the noise that occurs from day to day. Such safeguards include:

- **An Investment Policy Statement.** An IPS is a written document spelling out the key components of your financial situation and investment plan. During particularly strong or weak market environments, it can serve as a reminder of your reasons for structuring your portfolio the way you have. Whenever you are tempted to make a change to your investment plan, it's best to consult your IPS and remind yourself of the goals, needs and principles that initially drove your decision making. If a change you want to make conflicts with your IPS, you'll want to stop and assess if it really makes sense to move forward. If, however, your specific circumstances have actually changed, and your goals and needs are greater or less than they were before, a modification to your plan may make sense. In that case, a revision to the IPS should be made reflecting the change of circumstances and the corresponding change to your plan.

- **A rebalancing discipline.** As financial markets rise and fall, your portfolio's exposure to stocks, bonds, cash and other investments will tend to fluctuate as well. Over time, your overall target asset allocations can shift — leaving you with more money in stocks and less in bonds, for example. By rebalancing your portfolio back to its target allocations, you'll better control the level of risk in your portfolio and give yourself a system for minimizing emotional decision making.

Get The Help You Need

Building a comprehensive plan that coordinates investments with advanced planning requires a great deal of effort, expertise and time. Given all the components that a *360 Wealth Management* plan seeks to tie together, it's challenging for any one person — even a trained professional — to do everything alone.

For that reason, it's important to implement your wealth management plan with the help of a team of trusted professionals — experts who have knowledge across the entire range of wealth management disciplines and who can work together to coordinate all aspects of your financial situation.

Working as a team, these professionals can effectively address the various issues that today's investors face.

This *360 Wealth Management* approach is being used by many of today's most successful investors and families to make prudent financial decisions. And while some of those investors choose to work entirely on their own, we find that most prefer to work with a professional wealth advisor who is capable of devoting significant expertise and resources to the process.

CHAPTER 13

Selecting the Right Advisor

Now that you have an overview of *360 Wealth Management*, you must decide whether you want to do it yourself or work with a trusted wealth advisor.

This decision will come down to a number of factors — the level of expertise you possess in investment planning and advanced planning, as well as the amount of time you can dedicate to creating and maintaining a comprehensive wealth plan. Even if you do have the expertise and time, you will need to determine if you have the desire to add this responsibility to a list of other priorities, such as family, hobbies and travel.

Although some investors choose to manage their financial affairs by themselves, we have noticed that in recent years, many investors have increasingly looked to professional wealth advisors for guidance. Additionally, as individual investors' wealth increases, so does their desire to delegate to a wealth advisor.

Make no mistake: Choosing a wealth advisor is one of the most important decisions you will make. There are an enormous number of financial professionals out there who want to work with you. However, far too few offer the type of comprehensive, consultative approach that we have outlined in this book. If you believe that the

360 Wealth Management philosophy will help you make the smartest possible decisions about your future planning needs, then you will need to work with an advisor who has adopted this approach.

Benefits of Working With An Advisor

The challenges that have occurred in the financial markets in recent years have prompted many investors to seek professional help.

An experienced advisor can provide a number of benefits, including:

- **Expertise.** As we have seen, navigating financial markets is not an easy task. Additionally, the intricacies of wealth management — investments, estate planning, tax strategies, wealth preservation and other components — can make coordinating your planning needs a difficult job. One of the roles of a good advisor is to understand your needs and goals and then assemble the requisite expertise to address those needs and reach those goals. That expertise should ideally come from both the advisor and a team of trusted experts with whom the advisor works and closely coordinates.

- **Discipline.** Investors are often their own worst enemies — buying high, selling low and putting their financial plans in jeopardy. A professional advisor should have the knowledge, experience and objectivity to remain calm during volatile market environments, prevent investors from making emotional financial decisions and help them stay focused on their long-term objectives.

- **Time.** Delegating part of your financial affairs to an advisor can allow you to maximize your free time and spend it on those activities that you enjoy most. Of course, some investors enjoy spending time working on their investments and even their financial plans. And while that may be preferable for some, we find that most investors would prefer to pursue other interests beyond wealth management.

- **Perspective.** Advisors work with many clients who share similar financial concerns and issues. Over time this can help advisors gain valuable perspective about how to solve problems and capture opportunities in the most effective and creative ways. In addition, by working in collaboration with other professionals, advisors benefit by having a variety of different points of view examining the same client information.

Of course, in some instances, a professional advisor may not be necessary. If, for example, you have a modest amount of assets and your financial situation is extremely straightforward and easy for you to understand, you may not require the expertise that an advisor brings. In that case, you may be best served by building a well-diversified portfolio of low-cost mutual funds and periodically reviewing and rebalancing your asset allocation.

If your situation is more complex, however, an advisor may be able to add substantial value. To help you decide whether working with an advisor is a good option for you, consider the following questions:

- Are you in a position to spend a significant amount of time managing your financial affairs? If so, do you want to spend your free time in that way — or are there other interests you would rather pursue?

- What is your level of expertise about investments, tax management strategies, estate planning techniques, wealth protection options, charitable gifting tools and other key components of wealth management?

- How will you stay up-to-date with changes in the tax code, estate planning laws and other developments that could affect your future? How confident are you in your ability to consistently make the smartest possible decisions about your financial plan, year after year, in all the areas that are important to you and your family?

What to Look for in a Financial Advisor

Any financial advisor you work with must be able to bring significant value. Since your understanding of any advisor's process and how it corresponds to serving you will be essential, we've provided a list of key criteria to think about.

We have worked with hundreds of advisors over the years and have identified some of the factors that differentiate successful advisors from the rest of the pack. As you interview potential advisors, ask the following questions:

- **What professional designation(s) does the advisor have?** The single most important designation to look for when evaluating an advisor is whether or not he or she is an independent advisor. Independent advisors are legally required to act as a fiduciary — which means they must always put your interests as a client ahead of their own. In addition they must disclose all important information to you, including fees charged and conflicts of interest. In short, it is illegal for them to engage in any situation that would serve their interests over yours.

  Also, ask if the advisor has an advanced designation such as Certified Financial Planner™ (CFP®). A CFP® designation tells you that the advisor has received formal education and training on a wide variety of financial planning topics and has passed an exam testing their financial planning knowledge and skills. CFPs also are required to take continuing education courses each year to stay current on these issues. If the advisor is not a CFP, inquire about how many years he or she has been in the financial services industry. With non-CFPs, you'd like to see that they have at least five years' experience (and preferably more).

- **What is the advisor's compensation structure?** An advisor's compensation structure can tell you a great deal about what your experience working together may be like. There are three basic types of compensation structures: fee-only, fee-based, and commission-based.

– **Fee-only advisors** are entirely compensated by fees paid to them by their clients, usually structured as a percentage of the assets they manage.

– **Fee-based advisors** receive the majority of their compensation from client fees, but may also receive commissions on some products (such as life insurance or long-term care policies).

– **Commission-based brokers** receive their fees from commissions generated by buying or selling investment products for clients.

By working with a fee-only or fee-based advisor, it is more likely that your interests are aligned with theirs, as they are paid for advice, not for the sale of a financial product (except in the case of fee-based advisors as discussed above). Additionally, fee-based and fee-only advisors are able to avoid conflicts of interest because of the fee structure; commission-based advisors are only compensated when making trades in a client's account, so they have an inherent incentive to encourage buying and selling.

Advisors who adopt a *360 Wealth Management* philosophy fit into either the fee-only or fee-based camps. The advice they provide is based on what is in their client's best interest. For example, if it requires 10 hours or 20 hours a year to help you with your planning needs their compensation is the same. Essentially, you are paying for access to their time and wisdom versus purchasing a product or engaging in a transaction

• **What types of clients does the advisor serve?** Many advisors have a clearly defined type of client they serve. It might be broad-based (retirees, for example) or highly-focused (such as executives in the health care profession). Having a targeted approach offers two advantages. For one, it means they have specific knowledge and expertise in issues common to a certain category of client. Second, it means that if you are not a good fit for that advisor, he should tell you so and recommend another advisor.

- **Is the advisor consultative?** Perhaps the clearest sign of whether an advisor is consultative or not will occur the first time you meet. A consultative advisor will let you do plenty of talking about what you are looking for, and will ask you questions designed to identify what is really important to you as well as what specific issues you are concerned about. The best consultative advisors will have a formal process for uncovering those issues, such as the discovery process that we have highlighted in this book.

By contrast, a non-consultative advisor will most likely spend much of your first meeting talking rather than listening. But remember: An advisor's job is to do all he or she can to help you reach your most important goals. If you encounter an advisor who takes little interest in those issues from the start — or asks you just a handful of basic, investment-only questions — chances are the advisor is most interested in getting just enough information from you to recommend a specific product. He's probably not too concerned about understanding your personal and financial goals and helping you manage your entire future.

Another good indication that the advisor is consultative is if she uses a defined process for meeting with clients and helping them on a regular basis. Therefore, when you meet with an advisor, make sure to ask her to spell out her approach for working with clients, and decide if her answers indicate a consultative approach with regular meetings.

- **Does the advisor sell performance?** When an advisor you interview discusses his investment methodology, pay close attention. Does he highlight how much he's beaten the market lately or emphasize his ability to generate huge returns through a "specialized" or "proprietary" approach? If so, be wary. The promise of consistent market-beating returns (or suggestions along those lines) is a red flag. As you'll remember, decades of research show that accurately predicting the winning and losing investments, asset classes and markets year after year is hugely difficult — nearly impossible, really. An advisor who sells performance as the primary reason to work with him is likely to continually buy and sell products in your portfolio.

We've witnessed more of this performance-selling in recent years as the markets have been increasingly volatile. Many advisors today like to talk about the ability to offer "downside protection" and "alternative" techniques that will get clients in and out of the markets at just the right times. We think this is simply market timing disguised as risk management. Using these approaches, you may win — but the greater likelihood is that you will lose. Regardless, it's a huge gamble to take with your future.

If you believe (as we do) that the most prudent investment approach is to try and capture market rates of return, then it clearly makes sense to work with an advisor who is aligned with your thinking and investment philosophy.

- **Does the advisor work with other professionals to solve your biggest concerns?** As we've noted before, the full range of your wealth management concerns are diverse and complex. To effectively understand them in an integrated manner, an advisor needs to bring expertise and skilled resources to the process. In rare cases, an advisor may possess all the skills needed to build and maintain a comprehensive wealth management plan. Typically, however, you'll want to see that your advisor can coordinate the efforts of a team of trusted professionals — which should typically include a CPA, an estate planning attorney and an insurance specialist — to create truly comprehensive solutions.

- **What tools does the advisor use to maintain your wealth management plan?** Think about all the moving parts of a wealth management plan. Clearly, such a plan cannot be created once and put in a drawer. It needs to be monitored, reviewed and updated on a regular basis. That's why you need to know what tools and criteria an advisor uses to maintain clients' plans and keep them current.

  The advisor should be taking advantage of advanced technology such as financial planning software. You will also want to see that the advisor has a systematic, disciplined method for reviewing clients' objectives and risk tolerance, and rebalancing portfolios in order to keep the portfolio at the targeted allocation. Finally, ask if the advisor creates an Investment Policy Statement for each client.

  As mentioned earlier, an IPS should detail all the key components of your investment plan. Because of its ability to help keep investors on track, we believe an IPS is absolutely crucial for every investor.

- **Does the advisor have a clean record?** You can research an advisor's compliance record to see if he's ever been censured or received client complaints by going to the BrokerCheck feature on the Financial Industry Regulatory Authority's website (www.finra. org/Investors/ToolsCalculators/BrokerCheck). This site only covers advisors who work with a broker dealer. For independent advisors, go to the Investment Adviser Public Disclosure website (IAPD) at www.adviserinfo.sec.gov. If an advisor has any prior complaints or enforcement actions on his record, go back and ask the advisor for details about the situation and decide after that if you should consider working with him or her. For some investors with substantial wealth, having a background check run on a potential advisor can ensure that the advisor has not run afoul of financial regulatory agencies in the past, or has not been convicted of certain crimes.

The Next Step Is Yours

Whether you work with a financial advisor or go it alone, we firmly believe that the single most important move you can make today is to start implementing the concepts discussed in this book.

Take a minute to think again about your most important goals — the things you value on a deep and personal level, and the things you would like to achieve in order to live a comfortable, meaningful and satisfied life. Then think about all the important people in your life — your spouse or partner, your children or your parents — and the hopes and dreams you have for them, as well as any challenges that they face. Finally, consider any causes or issues that you care about and want to support, which might include anything from fighting global poverty to supporting your city's symphony orchestra.

When you think about all of this, one fact is illuminated: You can do an enormous amount of good for your family, your community and the world at large. Even if you never consider yourself wealthy, you can still make a huge impact and positively shape your life and the lives of others. What a fantastic position to be in! In the end, then, you have a responsibility to make smart decisions about your wealth so that it can do as much good as possible. You owe it to yourself and to the people and organizations you care about most to do the job right.

Ultimately, this is where *360 Wealth Management* can make all the difference. This process was designed with one goal in mind: to enable you to coordinate and comprehensively manage all the key parts of your finances, no matter how complex, in order to solve your biggest financial challenges and achieve everything that is important to you.

Over our decades of experience in the financial services, we've seen a lot of ideas and approaches come and go. But in all that time, we have never seen a smarter, more prudent or more effective way for investors to manage their wealth than *360 Wealth Management*. Its consultative process in which customized solutions are designed and coordinated by a team of experts has helped many successful families get exactly what they want out of their wealth.

The next step is yours. You have an opportunity to achieve a higher level of financial success than you may have thought possible, and have a higher level of confidence that your goals and aspirations will come to fruition. Seize this opportunity now to create benefits for yourself and those around you that could resonate for generations to come.

We wish you a lifetime of financial and personal success.

How to Lose Money

HARRY M. MARKOWITZ, PHD

1990 Nobel Prize Laureate in Economic Sciences and Member, Loring Ward Investment Committee

If you want to become an acknowledged Saint, it is best if you start by giving away all your money. If this prospect sounds too daunting, the following are four efficient suggestions for reducing your wealth. The first two may only lose most of it but the final two will make it all disappear.

The first advice toward achieving poverty on your way to Sainthood is to invest in the hottest stocks in the hottest sector: Buy auto stocks when the car is the latest new invention; purchase tech stocks when they are the "in" thing; invest in mortgage-based derivatives when all the "smart" money is doing the same. Under no circumstances should you read Charles Mackay's book *Extraordinary Popular Delusions and the Madness of Crowds*. Instead, just try your utmost to keep up with the thundering herd.

If you are too cautious to follow the preceding advice, here is some rock-solid, very sensible, traditional advice: Put all your money in some big, trusted company — like the one you work for, the one that already pays your salary — like Eastern Airlines, Penn Central, or Enron.

The aforementioned ways of losing money involve buying stocks traded on exchanges, such as the NYSE and NASDAQ. But if you do not want to invest in these, because you don't trust the guy on TV who barks advice at you, listen to your trusted neighbor or uncle who knows a brilliant investor who has figured out how to double your money in less than a year! I know of a guy like that: His name was Charles Ponzi.

Last, but not least, find a financial advisor who will take care of your money for you. To be sure to lose money and perfect your plan for poverty, do not work with an advisor such as recommended in this book. Instead, find an advisor who provides the added service of holding your money for you rather than having you keep it with a large, nationally recognized custodian that periodically sends, directly to you, reports of how your account is doing.

More generally, for optimal effect, just ignore the advice in this book.

Alex Potts

President and Chief Executive Officer, Loring Ward

Alex Potts is the President and CEO of Loring Ward Group Inc. and its affiliates, as well as the SA Funds – Investment Trust.

Potts founded and was President, Chief Executive Officer and Director of Loring Ward Securities Inc. (formerly Assante Capital Management Inc.). In addition, he served as Executive Vice President and General Manager of LWI Financial Inc. (formerly Assante Asset Management, Inc.). In 1999, Alex started the SA Funds – Investment Trust and was named President and Chief Executive Officer.

From 1990 – 2000, he served in various positions at Loring Ward and its predecessor firms, including Senior Vice President of Investment Operation.

Potts earned a Bachelor of Science degree in Economics from Santa Clara University.

Joni L. Clark, CFA, CFP®

Chief Investment Officer, Loring Ward

Joni L. Clark has advised clients on all aspects of investment strategy and portfolio risk management for two decades. Her clients have included affluent individuals and families, investment management organizations and large institutional pension funds.

As Chief Investment Officer of Loring Ward, she directs investment policy and portfolio management strategies for the company. She also chairs the company's Investment Committee.

Prior to joining Loring Ward in 2002, Clark held senior positions with some the country's most respected financial services firms. She began her career at Merrill Lynch PFS (1989-1991). She then worked as Vice President of Wilshire Associates (1991-1998), consulting for large public and corporate defined benefit plans, foundations and endowments, and institutional investment management firms. She also was a Managing Director at Legg Mason Institutional Advisors (1998-2000), overseeing client service for institutional client relationships. And she was a Senior Investment Consultant and Portfolio Manager at Enright Financial Consultants (2000-2002), a boutique investment management firm serving affluent individuals and families.

Clark received a Bachelor of Science degree in Finance in 1988, a Chartered Financial Analyst (CFA) designation in 1994, and became a Certified Financial Planner (CFP®) in 2004. She is a member of the CFA Institute, the Los Angeles Society of Financial Analysts, and the Financial Planning Association.

Steven J. Atkinson, CFS

Executive Vice President and Head of Advisor Relations,
Loring Ward

For more than fifteen years, Steve Atkinson has been dedicated to helping create a better experience for independent financial advisors so that they can create a world-class experience for their clients.

As an Executive Vice President at Loring Ward, Atkinson speaks frequently at client and advisor events and has personally coached over 100 advisors.

He is a graduate of the University of Nebraska at Omaha, with a Bachelor of Science degree in Finance and Investment Banking. He is also a Certified Fund Specialist (CFS).

ACKNOWLEDGEMENTS

It took the ideas, hard work and inspiration of many people to create this book. We especially want to thank Mark Klimek and William Chettle for all their help in writing, editing and organizing our thoughts. Eric Golberg made substantial and invaluable contributions to the chapters on Wealth Management. Thank you to Karen Parker for her careful editing and proofing, Matt Carvalho, Wynce Lam, and Sheldon McFarland provided the charts and data. Ed Robertson brought his creative talents to the layout and cover design. Chris Stanley, Nish Patel and Huong Nguyen provided legal and regulatory guidance. And thanks above all to all our colleagues at Loring Ward for their support and encouragement.

WEALTH SOLUTION GLOSSARY

Active Management — An investment strategy of actively buying and selling investments in an attempt to beat the return of the broad stock market (or other benchmark). Academics have reviewed historical fund performance data and found that few active mutual fund managers have been able to consistently achieve better investment returns than the broad stock market.

Annualized Return — The annualized return (not to be confused with average return) is a geometric average return that takes into account compounding during the year.

Asset Allocation — The proportions dedicated to asset classes (bonds, domestic stocks, international stocks, etc.) across an investor's portfolio. An asset allocation strategy should be based on an investor's willingness and ability to take risk.

Asset Class — An investment category such as bonds, stocks, real estate and cash. More specifically, asset classes can identify a specific subset of investments; for example, instead of simply classifying an investment as a bond, the investment can be labeled as a long term U.S. Government Bond.

Benchmark — An index for which investment performance can be compared. Investors often compare the performance of their stocks or mutual funds to the Dow Jones Industrial Average to see if they are outperforming the market or underperforming the market.

Bond — An investment in a company, government, or other entity's debt in which an investor gives the entity money, and in exchange the entity pays the investor interest (a coupon payment) at fixed time intervals and/or or repays the principal at a later date. An investor may buy a bond from the U.S. Government, U.S. Government Agencies, Corporations, international governments, and as well as several other entities.

Correlation — A statistical measurement showing how a stock or fund performs relative to another. Perfect positive correlation implies that as one stock or fund moves, either up or down, the other will move in the same direction. Alternatively, perfect negative correlation means that if one stock or fund moves up, the other will move down, or vice versa.

Diversification — Investing in a variety of investments with the goal of lowering the portfolio's risk by minimizing its exposure to any one stock, industry, asset class or country. The intention of diversification is to eliminate company-specific risk (unsystematic risk).

Exchange Traded Funds (ETFs) — Most commonly a fund whose goal is to track the performance of an index such as the Dow Jones Industrial Average. An ETF is similar to a mutual fund in that it typically contains many individual underlying holdings. In some ways however it is different than a mutual fund and more like a stock in that it can have options and can be bought and sold short throughout the trading day.

Emerging Markets Stock — Shares in the financial markets of a single, or a group, of developing countries.

Equity — An ownership interest; also referred to as stock.

Fixed Income — A debt or loan investment that pays an investor a "fixed income" or interest payment; also referred to as a bond.

Growth Stock — A stock that is expected to experience above average growth relative to its industry or the broad market.

Index Fund — A type of fund designed to track a market index such as the S&P 500 Index. The purpose of an index fund is to provide broad market exposure with low operating expenses and low turnover.

Inflation — Rising prices for goods and services. In years of inflation, it costs more dollars to purchase a similar item than it did the year before. The opposite of inflation is deflation, in which it costs fewer dollars to purchase a similar item than it did the year before.

International Stock — Shares in companies located outside the United States.

Large-Cap Stock — A stock with a market capitalization (see definition below) value of typically more than $10 billion. Large cap is an abbreviation of "large market capitalization."

Market Capitalization — The market value of a publicly traded company. The market capitalization is a value placed on a company that is based on its total number of shares and market price per share. The investment community uses this figure (as opposed to sales or total asset figures)to determine a company's size. Frequently referred to as "market cap."

Maturity — The time remaining on the life of a financial instrument, commonly a bond or certificate. Maturity often is used in the context of maturity date, which is the date when a bond's final payment is due.

Mutual Fund — An individual holding where money is pooled together from thousands of investors in order to buy stocks, bonds or other securities. One of the main advantages of owning mutual funds is that they give small investors access to diversified portfolios which would be difficult to create with a small amount of money. Each shareholder participates proportionally in the gain or loss of the fund.

Passive Management — An investment strategy that minimizes buying and selling investments. Passive strategies often attempt to mimic the performance of an index such as the S&P 500 or Dow Jones Industrial Average. Passive managers seek to minimize costs and avoid unnecessary risk.

Real Estate Investment Trusts (REITs) — An investment in one or more forms of real estate such as commercial, industrial, or residential real estate either through properties or mortgages. REITs trade similarly to a stock or Exchange Traded Fund (ETF), and often trade on major exchanges like the New York Stock Exchange.

Recession — A natural part of the economic cycle in which the economy shrinks. Technically, a recession is defined as two or more quarters (6 months) of negative economic growth.

Risk — The chance that an investment's actual return will be different than what is expected. Risk includes the possibility of losing some or all of the original investment. Risk is often measured with standard deviation which quantifies the amount of volatility in investment returns.

Risk Tolerance — The amount of uncertainty (including potential losses) an investor is willing to accept in their investment strategy.

S&P 500 — A stock market index comprised of 500 of some of the largest U.S. companies. It is often used as a benchmark and a gauge of the U.S. stock market.

Share — An ownership in a corporation or financial asset. Being a shareholder entitles the possessor to a proportional distribution in profits, if any are declared, in the form of dividends.

Small-Cap Stock — A stock with a market capitalization (see definition above) value of typically between $2 billion and $300 million. Small cap is an abbreviation of "small market capitalization."

Standard Deviation — Standard deviation measures the volatility of an investment's return over time. An investment with returns that vary greatly will exhibit higher standard deviation. Standard deviation is used by investors to gauge the amount of expected risk in an investment.

Stock — An investment that represents ownership in a corporation. Being a stockholder or shareholder entitles the possessor to a proportional distribution in profits, if any are declared, in the form of dividends.

Style — The specific asset class exposure of a stock, bond, or mutual fund. For example, Google's stock style is Large Growth, meaning that it is grouped into the asset class of large companies that experience relatively higher growth.

Systematic Risk — The inherent risk of investing in the stock market. Systematic risk cannot be reduced through diversification.

Turnover — A measure of the amount of change in fund holdings per year. Fund turnover can primarily be attributed to buying and selling holdings. Studies have shown that higher turnover typically reduces mutual fund performance.

Value Stock — A stock that trades at a price that is lower than expected given the performance of the company and key performance indicators of the stock itself.

Volatility — An observation of the movement in the price of an investment. For example, if the price of a stock moves up and down rapidly over short time periods, it has high volatility. If the price almost never changes over the same time period, it has low volatility. Volatility typically is measured in standard deviation or variance.

Unsystematic Risk — Individual stock investments contain business risks such as government regulation or unforeseen employee or factory risks. An investor can reduce this risk by diversifying — buying hundreds of different stocks in many different types of companies.

DISCLOSURES

NAREIT

"FTSE®" is a trade mark of the London Stock Exchange Group companies and is used by FTSE International Limited ("FTSE") under licence. "NAREIT" a trade mark of the National Association of Real Estate Investment Trusts ("NAREIT"). The NAREIT Equity REIT Index is calculated by FTSE. Neither FTSE nor NAREIT sponsor, endorse or promote this product and are not in any way connected to it and do no t accept any liability.

All intellectual property rights in the index values and constituent list vests in FTSE and NAREIT. Loring Ward Securities, Inc has obtained full licence from FTSE to use such intellectual property rights in the creation of this product.

Russell

Russell data Copyright © Russell Investments 1995-2012. All rights reserved.

Russell offers investment planning services and diversified funds to individual and institutional investors. Russell advises clients in more than 35 countries on the investment of approximately $786 billion in assets, and serves approximately 600 organizations and thousands of individuals through its investment management business. Today, $152 billion is invested in Russell funds globally.

This is a publication of Russell Investments. It should not be construed as investment advice. It is not a solicitation or recommendation to purchase any services of any organization unless otherwise noted. The contents are intended for general information purposes only, and you are urged to consult your own investment advisor concerning your own situation and any specific investment questions you may have. For further information about these contents, please contact Russell. The information contained herein has been obtained from sources that we believe to be reliable, but its accuracy and completeness are not guaranteed. Russell Investments reserves the right at anytime and without notice to change, amend, or cease publishing the information. It has been prepared solely for informative purposes. It is made available on an "as is" basis. Russell Investments does not make any warranty or representation regarding the information. Without prior written permission from Russell Investments, it may not be reproduced, in whole or in part, in any form, other than for your own personal, noncommercial use.

Russell Investments is a registered trademark of Russell Investments in the U.S. and/or other countries. Russell Investments is the owner of the trademarks, service marks and copyrights related to its indexes. Indexes are unmanaged and cannot be invested in directly.